KV-056-215

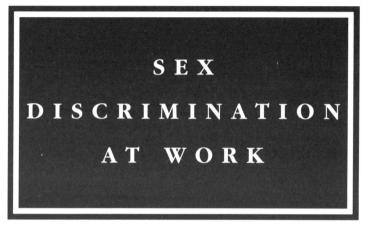

SEX DISCRIMINATION AT WORK

by

Robert Spicer
MA, Barrister

Lin Spicer
MEd

CLT PROFESSIONAL PUBLISHING
A DIVISION OF CENTRAL LAW TRAINING LTD

Published by
CLT Professional Publishing
A Division of Central Law Training Ltd
Wrens Court
52-54 Victoria Street
Sutton Coldfield
Birmingham
B72 1SX

ISBN 1 85811 038 6

Typeset by Dorchester Typesetting Group Ltd, Dorchester, Dorset
Printed in Great Britain by The Lavenham Press

Contents

Preface

The aim of this book is to examine the development of sex discrimination and equal pay law during the last 25 years. The current rules are complex and contradictory, and are based on five main sources, as follows:

1. *Statutes*   The Equal Pay Act 1970 and the Sex Discrimination Act 1975 are the main legislation in this field.
2. *Case law*   This book summarises approximately 100 leading cases which interpret and expand the statutes.
3. *European materials*   These include Treaties, Directives and European Court decisions which have had a dramatic effect on English law.
4. *Industrial tribunal procedure*   This is of crucial practical importance and includes rules as to time limits and levels of compensation.
5. *Internal codes and procedures relating to specific professions and employment*   Although these are not a part of the general law, they may have great significance for individuals. For example, a senior barrister was recently suspended from practice for three months for sexually harassing clients. Further, the provisions of such codes may have evidential significance.

An analysis of the leading 100 sex discrimination cases shows that developing trends have been most significant in the following areas:

- Pregnancy
- Retirement
- European law

Each of these areas has a separate chapter devoted to case law developments.

Although there is a very considerable overlap between European cases and topics dealt with in specific chapters, the European material has been separately organised so that readers may examine the role of the European Court as a separate matter.

This book does not aim to be exhaustive, nor to provide a detailed analysis of the statutory provisions. It sets out to discuss the significance of the leading cases and to identify trends, particularly in the area of pregnancy dismissals and the European Court.

Robert Spicer, MA, Barrister
Lin Spicer, MEd

Table of Cases Digested

Introduction

CHAPTER 1

Introduction

Background to the legislation

The main source of sex discrimination law is the Sex Discrimination Act 1975. This has now been overlaid with a mass of decided cases and with European materials. It remains the basis of UK rules on gender discrimination at work.

The origins of the 1975 Act lie in the principles set out by the Labour Party White Paper, *Equality for Women* (1974). That Paper drew extensively from US experience in dealing with discrimination. It was not concerned with private relationships, but rather with: "The status of women in society, the disabilities and disadvantages imposed upon women, and their consequences". In a nutshell, the Act made discrimination on the grounds of sex, marital status or by way of victimisation unlawful in a comprehensive range of activities in the employment and social fields, and set up the Equal Opportunities Commission.

Sections 1–5 of the Act deal with the principal definitions of discrimination. Sections 6–10 specifically cover discrimination in employment.

Definitions

Discrimination can occur in two principal ways:

1. Overt, direct discrimination, where an employer denies a person the opportunity of employment because of his or her gender. This is unlawful in all cases, except where the requirement for a person of a particular gender is a "genuine occupational qualification". This phrase has been the object of a number of decided cases.
2. Indirect discrimination, which generally arises where an employer attaches a pre-condition to an opportunity which, at first sight, appears to apply equally to either sex, but which in fact imposes a barrier against one sex because a person of that sex is less likely to meet the precondition.

It is important to note that the terms "direct" and "indirect" are not used in the legislation. Their differences, and precise meaning, are nevertheless important.

Direct discrimination

This occurs when an employer, in relation to a woman, "on the ground of her sex, treats her less favourably than he treats or would treat a man".

Indirect discrimination

In general terms, this arises when, in relation to a woman, an employer applies to her a requirement or condition which he applied or would apply equally to a man which:

- is such that the proportion of women who can comply with it is considerably smaller than the proportion of men who can comply;
- he cannot show to be justifiable, irrespective of the sex of the person to whom it is applied; and
- is to her detriment because she cannot comply with it.

Acts qualifying as discrimination

Section 6 of the Act lists the following:

1. Arrangements made for the purpose of determining who should be offered employment.
2. Terms on which employment is offered.
3. Refusing or deliberately omitting to offer employment.
4. Affording access to opportunities for promotion, transfer or training, or to any other benefits, facilities or services, or by refusing or deliberately omitting to afford access to them.
5. Dismissal or subjecting to detriment.

Note that this applies equally to discrimination against men. The burden of proof is upon the employee making the complaint. Only like cases can be compared.

SEX DISCRIMINATION

1. Comparing like with like

Schmidt v *Austicks Bookshops Ltd* (1971)

A woman cannot successfully claim unlawful sex discrimination on the grounds of a rule which forbids women employees to wear trousers. She must show that the circumstances of her case are "the same or not materially different" from those of the man she is comparing herself with.

Miss Schmidt worked in a bookshop which employed 20 women and 2 men. In order to uphold their public image the employer had a rule forbidding female bookshop staff from wearing trousers. This rule was not imposed on the men and Miss Schmidt thought that this rule therefore discriminated against her.

The EAT found that because there was no comparable restriction on the men, nor could there be, no discrimination occurred. Because, in the words of section 5(3), their circumstances were not "the same or materially different", Miss Schmidt was not able to compare her case with that of the men.

2. Man with long hair

Smith v *Safeway plc* (1994)

S, a male delicatessen assistant, was dismissed because he let his hair grow into a ponytail. A female worker with the same hairstyle would not have been dismissed. S complained of unfair dismissal.

The employer argued that different rules relating to standards of smartness could be applied to men and women, relying on the principle stated in *Schmidt* v *Austicks Bookshops*. The EAT ruled that to make a distinction between men and women as to the length of hair permitted was clearly detrimental and unfair to men. Further, it was inconsistent with the purposes of the 1975 Act.

Note, however, that Pill J dissented from the judgment. In his view, employers were entitled to lay down reasonable requirements as to the way in which employees presented themselves at work if, for example, they came into contact with the public.

3. Man with earrings

McConomy v *Croft Inns Ltd* (1992)

It is unlawful discrimination to bar a man from working in a pub for wearing earrings.

4. Proof of discrimination

S Moberley v *Commonwealth Hall (University of London)* (1977)
A prima facie case of discrimination is raised when an employee has evidence which points to a distinction in treatment between herself and that accorded to a man. However, an employer has good defence to the claim if he has good evidence that the reason for the distinction was not to do with her sex but based on other grounds.

A study room in the Commonwealth Hall, which housed students, was normally kept locked. In her capacity as part-time relief porter Miss Moberley had the use of a master key to the room. As she was also a full-time student at the University of London this was very useful to her. The authorities said they were not satisfied with Miss Moberley's competence and responsibility to hold a key and took it away from her. The key was put into the custody of the main porter and Miss Moberley claimed that this put her at a disadvantage as against a male employee, in that he had a key and she did not and this amounted to unlawful sex discrimination.

The EAT found that the the industrial tribunal had been correct in finding that the authority's reason for the different and less favourable treatment was based not on sex but on their opinion of Miss Moberley's suitability as a key holder.

5. Selection arrangements: interview questions

V Saunders v *Richmond Upon Thames BC* (1977)
Asking certain types of question at an interview is not sex discrimination. It depends on whether the employer intended to discriminate in asking the question or in his reaction to the question.

Miss Saunders was asked the following questions at her interview with the council:

> "Do you think men respond as well to a woman golf professional as to a man?"

> "Are there any women golf professionals in clubs?"

> "So you'd be blazing a trail would you?"

> "If some of the men were causing trouble on the tee do you think you would be able to control this?"

When she was not offered a final interview she lodged a sex discrimination complaint.

It was held that although the questions an employer asks at the interview are an indicator of his thinking, simply to ask these kinds of questions does not of itself constitute discrimination. Under section 6(1)(a) of the 1975 Act the applicant would have to prove that the questions were asked with the intent to discriminate and this Miss Saunders had not done.

6. "Any other benefits": minor differences

Automotive Products Ltd v *Peake* (1977)
Minor differences of treatment are not grounds for complaint even if they do slightly disadvantage one sex. The women at the factory where Mr Peake worked were allowed to leave five minutes earlier than the men and he claimed that this was a "benefit" from which he was excluded on grounds of sex. His claim was rejected by the Court of Appeal. The latin maxim *de minimis non curat lex* applied. A "benefit" is no more than an "advantage" and although Mr Peake had suffered a loss of advantage the infringement was too small to be recognised by the law.

7. "Any other benefits": "provision in relation to . . . retirement"

Garland v *British Rail Engineering* (1982)
Although retirement and death benefit provisions can be apportioned unequally between the sexes according to section 6(4) of the 1975 Act, a benefit such as cheap rail travel, which is allowed equally to employees' spouses whether they are male or female, when it is made available after retirement is not such a retirement benefit. It therefore amounts to unlawful sex discrimination to withdraw a cheap travel facility from female employees' husbands while retaining it for male employees' wives.

Cheap rail travel was allowed to spouses of British Rail employees during the employees' employment and after their retirement. However, as an economy measure this facility was withdrawn from former female employees' husbands although it was retained for former male employees' wives. When Mrs Garland complained that this discriminated against her on grounds of sex, British Rail argued that this concession was a "provision in relation to retirement" under section 6(4) and therefore was exempt from the anti-discrimination rules.

The EAT held that there was no exemption under section 6(4) as, although the withdrawal of the concession only affected female employees on their retirement, it was not a "provision in relation to retirement" but was an extension of a right which existed during employment. The case was referred to the House of Lords which referred the matter to the European

Court of Justice. It was held that "Where an employer (though not bound to do so by contract) provides special travel facilities for former male employees to enjoy after their retirement this constitutes discrimination within the meaning of Article 119 against former female employees who do not receive the same facilities."

8. Mobility clause: justification

Meade-Hill and another v *British Council* (1995)
Ms M, having been promoted by the British Council, her employer, was instructed to accept a variation in her contract of employment. The new contract contained a mobility clause which required her to work in such part of the United Kingdom as the employer required.

Ms M would not have been willing to move if required to do so because her husband earned more than she did. She sought a declaration that the clause amounted to indirect sex discrimination in breach of the 1975 Act, and was unenforceable under section 77(2). That section provides, in summary, that a term in a contract of employment which is unlawful under the 1975 Act by reasons of discrimination is not void but is unenforceable against the party being discriminated against. Thus, where a term contains benefits to the complainant, it can be enforced against other parties to the contract.

The judge at first instance dismissed the application. He ruled that in the absence of a concrete factual situation in which the council sought to apply the clause, the question whether it discriminated unfairly was speculative. The applicant appealed to the Court of Appeal which made the following points:

1. A higher proportion of women than men are secondary earners.
2. Accordingly, a higher proportion of women than men would find it impossible in practice to comply with an employer's instruction which involved moving house.
3. Therefore, the mobility clause in the present case amounted to indirect discrimination for the purposes of the 1975 Act.
4. The clause amounted to an application of a requirement detrimental to women which amounted to unlawful indirect sex discrimination.
5. The clause was unenforceable unless justified by the employer.
6. The appeal should be allowed and the matter remitted to the county court for consideration whether there was a defence of justification.

Equal Opportunities Commission

The Commission was created by the 1975 Act. It has the following duties:

- To work towards the elimination of sex discrimination
- To promote equality of opportunity between women and men
- To review the law and advise the Home Secretary on possible amendments

The Commission's powers which enable it to fulfil these duties are as follows:

1. The undertaking of formal investigations into discriminatory practices which are unsuitable to be dealt with on an individual basis.
2. Financial support for individuals who complain of sex discrimination.
3. The issue of Codes of Practice – these do not have the force of law but may be used in evidence at industrial tribunals.
4. Examination of areas of policy which are not specifically covered by the 1975 Act but which may have implications for sex discrimination. These include:
   - Social security
   - Taxation
   - Maternity rights.

5. The issue of non-discrimination notices, where as the result of a formal investigation the EOC concludes that there has been a breach of the law.
6. Research funding.
7. Applications for injunctions in, for example, the following circumstances:
   - Where an advertisement shows an intention to discriminate
   - Where an employee has been instructed to discriminate
   - Where a person puts pressure on another to discriminate.

Key problem areas

- Meaning of "indirect discrimination"
- Comparison between genders
- Discrimination against men
- Evidential problems: burden of proof
- Interview questions: implication of discrimination
- Minor differences in treatment
- Meaning of "any other benefits"

Meaning of Discrimination

Direct discrimination
1. Detriment: benefits, facilities or services
2. Detriment: less favourable rules on overtime

Sexual harassment
1. Amount of compensatory award
2. Whether amounting to discrimination
3. Detriment
4. Harassment not disputed by employer; duty to prevent further acts of harassment; burden of proof

Requirement or condition of employment
1. Justification: seniority rule
2. Condition with which fewer women can comply: age requirement
3. Only part-time employees made redundant
4. Advert for graduate aged 27-35: whether discriminatory against mature female students
5. Requirement with which fewer women than men could comply: whether discrimination made out; whether requirement reasonable; test to apply

Indirect discrimination
1. Redundancy selection: part-time employees first under "last in, first out"
2. Insisting on full-time working
3. Requirement or condition with which fewer women can comply

Constructive dismissal: pictures of nude women displayed in workplace; whether adverse treatment on grounds of sex

Unfair dismissal: continuous employment: whether qualifying requirements amount to indirect sex discrimination

Less favourable treatment: female nurse refusing to wear cap: male nurses not required to do so

Exceptions and exclusions
1. Genuine occupational qualification: preservation of decency; woman in state of undress
2. Work outside Great Britain
3. Doctor not appointed as general practitioner: whether "employment" statutory procedure

Key problem areas

CHAPTER 2

Meaning of Discrimination

Direct discrimination

I. Detriment: benefits, facilities or services

Calder v James Finlay Corporation Ltd (1989)

It amounts to a "detriment" for the purposes of unlawful discrimination where it is a requirement of a mortgage subsidy scheme that an applicant should be a man and a female cannot obtain the mortgage subsidy benefit under the scheme's rules.

From 1975 until 1981 Mrs Calder was employed by James Finlay Corporation Ltd, which operated a mortgage subsidy scheme. All eleven of the male employees received a mortgage subsidy but the eight women employees did not. When Mrs Calder applied for a subsidy she was told she was not eligible. On leaving the defendants' employ in 1981 she complained that she had been discriminated against on grounds of sex. Because her claim had not been presented within three months of the date when the act complained of was done, it was rejected.

The EAT, on appeal, held that there had been a continuing discrimination against Mrs Calder which was to be treated as having been done at the end of her employment. Therefore her complaint had been made within the time limit and should have been allowed.

2. Detriment: less favourable rules on overtime

Jeremiah v Ministry of Defence (1979)

A pre-condition to unpleasant overtime work done by men is a "detriment" within section 6(2)(b) of the 1975 Act when the same condition is not imposed on women.

"Colour bursting" shells were made at the munitions factory where Mr Jeremiah worked. These contained red or orange dye which was given off when they exploded and were used in target practice. As nobody liked working in the colour bursting shop the Ministry of Defence had a system under which anybody who wanted to do overtime had to do a stint in it. However, this condition applied only to men. Women were excused work in there because they objected to using the communal showers and the dye would ruin their hair. Mr Jeremiah complained that he was discriminated against because of this one-sided pre-condition on overtime work.

The Court of Appeal found that the condition was a "detriment" under section 6(2)(b) and was unlawful being on grounds of sex (by way of direct discrimination).

Sexual harassment

1. Amount of compensatory award

Wileman v *Minilec Engineering Ltd* (1988)

An award of £50 compensation for sexual harassment over a period of four-and-a-half years has been upheld by the EAT. Miss Wileman complained of sexual harassment over that period by one of her employer's directors. The tribunal found that this harassment had consisted of salacious remarks and physical harassment but it awarded her only £50 on the grounds that the harassment did not upset her and was a detriment only in the sense of being a minor irritation. It also took into account the fact that she wore clothes to work which on occasion were "scanty and provocative". The tribunal also found that although her employer had purported to dismiss her on grounds of redundancy it was actually because of her threat to bring proceedings for sexual harassment and therefore she had been unlawfully victimised.

On the grounds that she would have been made redundant within a matter of weeks anyway, she was awarded four weeks' pay in compensation. The employer sought to bring fresh evidence at the EAT hearing that Miss Wileman had posed for a national newspaper in a flimsy costume after the tribunal hearing. It was decided that the respondents would not be permitted to call fresh evidence as it was not likely to have an important influence on the result of the case.

The tribunal had been entitled to take into account the fact that the appellant wore scanty and provocative clothes on occasion and had therefore been correct in awarding £50 compensation. The award of four weeks wages was also correct as there was evidence before the tribunal that there was a redundancy situation and that the appellant was the person who would have been selected.

2. Whether amounting to discrimination

Wadman v *Carpenter Farrer Partnership* (1993)

A claim of sex discrimination was brought by W on the ground that she had been subjected to sexual harassment of various kinds. Her claim was dismissed by the tribunal, which stated: "even if we were able to accept the evidence of the applicant in its totality, we believe that whilst it certainly amounted to sexual harassment we do not believe that the conduct amounted to sexual discrimination and we therefore find the application fails". **W appealed.**

The appeal was allowed and the case remitted to a new tribunal. There was no way in which the thinking of the tribunal in the present case could be analysed. Since its decision contained no findings of primary fact and no sufficient direction in law from which the principles the tribunal had in mind could be ascertained, it would be set aside.

3. Detriment

Porcelli v *Strathclyde Regional Council* (1986)

The council employed three female laboratory technicians at a school. Two of them left and were replaced by males. P, the remaining female, alleged that she was subjected to a campaign of sexual harassment by the two men. The object of the campaign was to force her to leave.

P was transferred to another school at her own request. Her claim of unlawful discrimination was rejected by the tribunal, which found that P had been discriminated against by the two men; that the two men would have been equally unpleasant to a male colleague whom they disliked; and that, therefore, the men's employer could not be said to have treated P less favourably than they would have treated a man.

P's appeal to the EAT was allowed on the ground that the tribunal below should first have considered the question of sexual harassment. The council appealed to the Court of Session. That court dismissed the appeal, making the following points:

1. Section 1(1)(e) of the 1975 Act was concerned solely with the treatment of an employee, not the motive for that particular treatment.
2. Since part of the treatment of P was meted out only because she was a woman, the tribunal should first have asked itself whether there had been sexual harassment.
3. Since there had been such harassment, then P had been treated less favourably than a man.

4. Harassment not disputed by employer; duty to prevent further acts of harassment; burden of proof

Enterprise Glass Co v *Miles* (1990)

If there was no doubt over the fact of sex discrimination at work, then the legal burden was on the employer to show that it had taken reasonable steps to prevent such a course of conduct being continued by its employee.

After another employee repeatedly made suggestive remarks to A, she complained to her employer. The employer reprimanded him and told him that if it did not stop he would be given a formal written warning. He was promoted to supervisor in the same department as A shortly afterwards. He continued to make suggestive remarks to her.

After complaining again to her employer she was told to ignore his behaviour. She complained of sexual harassment by the employee to an industrial tribunal and claimed that the employer was liable for his conduct under section 41(1) of the 1975 Act. That section states, in paraphrase, that the principle of vicarious liability applies to sex discrimination in employment. Anything done by an employee during the course of employment is regarded, for the purposes of the Act, as being done by the employer, whether or not it was done with the employer's knowledge or approval.

Since the sexual harassment of A was not disputed before the tribunal by the employer, the tribunal held that it was guilty under section 41(1) because it had failed to take sufficient steps to prevent such conduct by its employee.

The employer's appeal was dismissed.

● The fact of discrimination was not in issue.
● Therefore by reason of section 41(1), the legal burden shifted to the employer to prove that it had taken such steps as were legally practicable to prevent the employee from continuing such a course of conduct.
● The employer had failed to establish a defence to the allegation of discrimination.

Requirement or condition of employment

1. Justification: seniority rule

Steel v *Union of Post Office Workers and the General Post Office* (1977)

An employer must prove that a discriminatory condition is necessary and not just convenient to the business in order to justify indirect discrimination. In order to see whether a method of work allocation whereby work is allocated according to seniority is really necessary, or whether some other system could be devised, the rule must be tested.

Traditionally, postal rounds were allocated according to seniority because some rounds are good for a postman and others less so. Women could not compete with men for seniority until 1975 as they were not permitted full-time status. After this was changed in 1975, women could only gain seniority with men beginning in 1975. Therefore a man (or woman) who joined in 1975 could have equal seniority with any existing female employee at that time regardless of her total service to date.

A man who joined just before 1975 would be ahead on seniority. Mrs Steel, who had been in Post Office employment since 1961, applied for a particularly desirable round but was rejected in favour of a man who had joined the Post Office in 1973.

When she complained she was told that under the rules on seniority the male employee was the most senior. She lodged a claim under the Sex Discrimination Act.

The case had to be remitted for consideration of the proper legal tests:

- Mrs Steel's employer had applied the seniority rule, a condition which effectively barred her from access to a postal round.
- She had been indirectly discriminated against as this was a condition which fewer women could comply with than men.
- It depended on whether the Post Office could justify it as to whether it was unlawful or not.
- Mere convenience is not sufficient.
- An employer has to show that the condition is necessary to his business in order to justify indirect discrimination.

The industrial tribunal had to look into the question of whether the Post Office really needed that particular rule of seniority to determine postal rounds or whether some other method of allocation might be equally good.

2. Condition with which fewer women can comply: age requirement

B.M. Price v *Civil Service Commission* (1977)
The legal test when assessing whether an employer is imposing a condition with which fewer women than men "can comply," is whether fewer women

can in practice comply. The test is decided on the basis of general knowledge, experience and practice, not by whether women can physically comply. If an age limit for application for a job produces an unequal proportion of eligible female applicants then it unlawfully discriminates. This is the effect of an age limit of 28, as many women are involved in bringing up a family at that age and they do not generally look for employment again until they are in their mid-30s.

An advertisement for people to apply to become Executive Officers was placed by the Civil Service Commission. The age range imposed for applications was from $17\frac{1}{2}$ to 28 years of age.

Mrs Price, who was 36, complained of unlawful sex discrimination, basing her claim on the argument that women up to the age of 28 were often involved in bringing up a family. Therefore the proportion of women who could comply with the age requirement was reduced to a level which was considerably smaller than the proportion of men who could comply.

The Civil Service replied that the number of women in the female population who could apply if they wished was not affected by their age limit. It was irrelevant whether or not they chose to have children.

The EAT found in favour of Mrs Price in that her argument was based on practicality.

- "Can comply" in section 1(1)(b) had to be interpreted in the light of experience, knowledge and practice.
- The legal test was "can proportionately fewer women under 28 meet the age requirement in practice?" The age limit of 28 years did discriminate when the unavoidable fact that many women are involved in bringing up a family until their mid-30s was taken into account.
- The case was remitted to a different tribunal for consideration of the facts in the light of the proper legal test.

3. Only part-time employees made redundant

Bhudi v *IMI Refiners* (1994)
Section 1(1)(b) of the 1975 Act was not required by EC law to be construed in such a way as to disregard the express provision requiring the application of a "requirement or condition".

Women working as part-time cleaners were administered differently from general service cleaners who were male and worked full time. When the part-time out-of-office-hours cleaning was contracted out, the women were made redundant.

The industrial tribunal held that no relevant requirement or condition had been applied within section 1(1)(b) of the Act and that the women had been dismissed because they were administered by the personnel department and cleaned outside office hours. Their claim for indirect discrimination was dismissed. The EAT allowed the women's appeal and remitted the case to the tribunal. The women could not establish indirect discrimination without showing that a requirement or condition had been applied pursuant to section 1(1)(b); the tribunal had not addressed the questions of whether a requirement or condition was such that the proportion of women who complied with it was considerably smaller than the proportion of men who complied with it.

4. Advert for graduate aged 27–35: whether discriminatory against mature female students

University of Manchester v *Jones* (1993)

It could be a requirement or condition within section 1(1)(b) of the 1975 Act that a job candidate needed to be within a particular age range without it being indirectly discriminatory on the grounds of sex.

The post of careers adviser at Manchester University was advertised. This advert stated that the person appointed would be a graduate, preferably 27–35 years of age. J was aged 46 and had obtained a degree as a mature student. She applied for the post but was not selected for interview. It was explained by the head of department, in writing, that a younger candidate was required to balance the number of older people on the staff.

J brought a complaint of unlawful sex discrimination contrary to section 1(1)(b). She argued that the age requirement discriminated against women who obtained their degrees as mature students.

The tribunal found that the age range was a condition or requirement within section 1(1)(b) and not merely a preference and that it was not justifiable and therefore discriminatory. The university appealed to the EAT. This appeal was upheld.

J appealed; the university cross-appealed; both were dismissed. The industrial tribunal's decision that the university had applied a condition or requirement in specifying an age range was one of fact which could not be disturbed. On the assumption that J proved the necessary facts the tribunal had been entitled to hold that the age requirement was discriminatory.

However, all male and female graduates with the necessary experience made up the correct "pool" or relevant population for comparison and therefore in taking the pool to be graduates who had undertaken degrees as mature students the industrial tribunal had erred. It had answered the wrong question. The appeal tribunal had correctly reversed its decision. Also, although the industrial tribunal had been correct in construing "justifiable" in section 1(1)(b)(ii) as requiring an objective balance between the discriminatory effect of the condition and the reasonable needs of the person applying the condition, this balancing exercise had not been carried out correctly.

5. Requirement with which fewer women than men could comply: whether discrimination made out; whether requirement reasonable; test to apply

Briggs v North Eastern Education and Library Board (1990)
B was an assistant science teacher. She coached badminton in the afternoons after school on a voluntary basis. She was promoted, conditional upon her written agreement to carry out additional duties; these included an agreement "to assist with extra-curricular school games". She continued with the badminton coaching in fulfilment of her new contractual duty.

In 1984 she adopted a baby. When she returned to school she changed the after school badminton coaching to lunchtimes. She stated that she intended to do so until her child reached school age. She agreed to reintroduce the badminton coaching to after school for one hour, one day a week. However, she refused to take the classes at a local leisure centre two miles from the school.

B confirmed at a disciplinary hearing on 1 May 1985 that she could not commit herself to regular after school coaching. She was prepared to take badminton coaching at lunchtimes and local league matches after school. Lunchtime coaching was considered to be only supplementary to after-school practice. The use of the leisure facilities was seen as important and B was informed by the disciplinary authority that she had unilaterally changed the basis upon which her promotion had been awarded. Her pay was reduced to the previous level.

The industrial tribunal found that she had made out a prima facie case of indirect discrimination. The appeal was upheld and the decision quashed. The tribunal had been correct in finding that a requirement had been applied to her which was such that the proportion of women who could comply with it was smaller than the proportion of men who could comply with it, and that because of her failure to do so she had suffered a detriment. However, the tribunal had erred in law in finding that the employer had not shown that the requirement was justifiable.

If the test in *Hampson* was applied, the employer's requirement that coaching should be carried out after school was a reasonable need which justified its discriminatory effect. The tribunal had come to a decision which no reasonable tribunal could have reached.

Indirect discrimination

I. Redundancy selection: part-time employees first under "last in, first out"

(1) Clarke v Eley (IMI) Kynoch Ltd and (2) Eley (IMI) Kynoch Ltd v Powell (1983)

When the greater proportion of part-time workers are women, it is unlawful sex discrimination to make part-time workers redundant first when implementing redundancies. However, even if it makes more women than men redundant it is not unlawful sex discrimination to operate a "last in, first out" policy.

Mrs Clarke and Mrs Powell worked in a Birmingham munitions factory which employed 60 part-time women and 140 full-time men. Mrs Clarke had turned down the opportunity to go full-time some years previously.

When they were selected for redundancy because of their part-time status they claimed that their selection was discriminatory against them as fewer women could comply with the condition of being full-time than men. This therefore caused them a detriment. (The period from when Mrs Clarke turned down the full-time position was sufficient for her to qualify to make a claim.) It was necessary to make the comparison at the time the complaint was made and at this time the company had imposed a condition with which Mrs Clarke and Mrs Powell could not comply.

In order to justify this indirect discrimination against the women the company had to show that the condition was reasonable, not whether it was absolutely necessary. To select women for redundancy because they were part-time, although convenient, was not reasonable. It was arbitrary and therefore unlawfully discriminatory. What was reasonable was to impose a regime of "last in, first out'. Although this too was arbitrary it was the most accceptable criterion.

The women also claimed compensation for unfair dismissal and it was held that it was unfair in the circumstances of this case as the company knew of the possibility of unfairness at the time the decision to dismiss them was taken.

2. Insisting on full-time working

Home Office v *Holmes* (1984)

The ruling by the EAT that it may be unlawful to insist that women work full-time in some circumstances has the effect of giving some women the legal right to work part-time only.

Ms Holmes was employed by the Home Office as an officer in the immigration and nationality department of the Civil Service. Whilst she was on maternity leave with her second child she wrote to her employer asking for permission to return to work in a part-time capacity as she was a single parent and therefore the task of bringing up two very young children was difficult. She had a contract of employment with a standard clause requiring her to work full-time.

The Home Office said there were no part-time posts within her grade and that she was legally entitled only to return to the full-time post she had previously held. Once Ms Holmes was back at work full-time she submitted a claim to an industrial tribunal that the Home Office's insistence that she work full-time amounted to an act of unlawful discrimination against her.

The "condition or requirement" which the Home Office had imposed on her work was one with which it was more difficult for women to comply than men, as women are more often involved in bringing up a family which makes full-time work more difficult. She also argued that there was no real justification for the Home Office requiring her to work full-time: there was no commercial case for it and even if there was, the Home Office had not made one out. The Home Office argued that no "detriment" had been suffered by Ms Holmes. It was not enough to say that she had been discriminated against and that the loss or detriment was the discrimination itself. She would have to show that she had lost reputation or money or suffered hurt feelings or some other detriment as a result of discrimination. It was also argued on behalf of the Home Office that full-time work was self-evidently justifiable and was standard throughout the industry.

All the points raised by Ms Holmes were accepted by the industrial tribunal, supported by the EAT and the Home Office's arguments in their defence rejected. Since the requirement to work full-time was a "requirement or condition" under section 1(1)(b) of the Act and as fewer women than men could comply with this condition, then it resulted in detriment to Ms Holmes. It was not enough for the Home Office to say that because the industry as a whole was organised on a full-time basis then it was justifiable in a particular case. The Home Office must produce evidence as to why the requirement is justified in a particular case and it had failed to do this.

3. Requirement or condition with which fewer women can comply

Greater Glasgow Health Board v *Carey* (1988)

Although the proportion of women who can comply with the requirement that a health visitor must work a five-day week is considerably smaller than the proportion of men who can comply, regard must be had to administrative efficiency.

On her return to work from maternity leave, Mrs Carey, a health visitor, asked her employer if she could work a full day for two or three days a week because of problems with child care arrangements. Mrs Carey's employer was prepared to offer part-time work but only on the basis of five-day working. She complained that this amounted to indirect sex discrimination. When her complaint was upheld by the industrial tribunal her employer appealed to the EAT.

The tribunal was right to find that the five-day week requirement was such that a smaller proportion of women than men could comply with it, but it had failed to take into account the administrative efficiency of the service.

The tribunal found, further, that the employer was justified in insisting that in order to enable the work of a health visitor to be carried out efficiently, a five-day week was essential.

Constructive dismissal: pictures of nude women displayed in workplace; whether adverse treatment on grounds of sex

Stewart v *Cleeveland Guest (Engineering)* (1994)

When S made a complaint to her employer about the display of pictures of nude women at her workplace he failed to respond in any way as in his view the pictures were not offensive. The pictures were removed after a complaint from S's union representative.

Following a deputation of female employees stating that they did not object to the pictures, S resigned. She complained of constructive dismissal and sex discrimination. Her complaint of constructive dismissal was upheld by the tribunal as her employers had failed to protect her from hostility from other employees and had failed to deal properly with her complaint. However, it was considered that a man who complained would have been treated in the same way and therefore the industrial tribunal rejected her claim of sex discrimination.

S's appeal to the EAT was dismissed. In each case it was a matter of fact for the tribunal to decide whether an applicant had been treated less favourably on grounds of her sex. The tribunal's finding that S had not suffered sex discrimination because a male employee would have been treated in the same way was not perverse and the tribunal had directed itself correctly in law.

Unfair dismissal: continuous employment: whether qualifying requirements amount to indirect sex discrimination

R v *Secretary of State for Employment, ex p Seymour-Smith and Perez* (1994)

S and P, who had been employed for less than two years at the dates of their dismissals by their respective employers, sought judicial review of the Unfair Dismissal (Variation of Qualifying Period) Order 1985. They claimed that as the proportion of women who could comply with the requirement was smaller than the proportion of men it was therefore indirectly discriminatory.

The application was dismissed. Since it had not been shown that the Secretary of State did not have power to make the Order, certiorari quashing the 1985 Order would not be granted. As the proportion of women who could comply was 89.1% of the proportion of men who could comply and was therefore not "considerably smaller", S and P had failed to show that the qualifying period discriminated against women.

If the claims had merit, they might have provided a cause of action for damages on the basis of *Francovich* v *Italian Republic* for failure to implement the EEC Equal Treatment Directive. If the requirement had been proved to be discriminatory, the Secretary of State had failed to establish objective justification.

Less favourable treatment: female nurse refusing to wear cap: male nurses not required to do so

Burrett v *West Birmingham Health Authority* (1994)

A nurse who was transferred to a different nursing position because she refused to wear a cap as part of her uniform brought a claim of unlawful sex discrimination. Male nurses who were also required to wear uniforms were not required to wear caps. The cap was considered by the nurse to be demeaning and undignified. It was accepted that the cap was not supplied as a matter of hygiene and served no practical purpose.

The tribunal held that a male nurse who refused to wear his uniform would have been treated in exactly the same way and rejected her claim. It was held that the tribunal had not erred because a male nurse would have been treated in the same way even though his uniform was different. What constitutes "less favourable treatment" is a question of fact for the tribunal and is not dependent upon the applicant's subjective belief. The nurse's appeal was dismissed.

Exceptions and exclusions

1. Genuine occupational qualification: preservation of decency; woman in state of undress

Sisley v *Britannia Security Systems Ltd* (1983)

An employer can refuse to employ men where a job does not directly require women to work in a state of undress, but it is inevitably incidental to the work.

A system was operated by Britannia Security to monitor an installation. During the 12 hours' shiftwork which was involved, employees would undress and sleep during their rest period. There were rest facilities provided at the site. To preserve decency in a situation where otherwise men and women would mix in close proximity in a state of undress, the company only employed women.

Mr Sisley made a claim for compensation under the 1975 Act after being rejected for such work. The EAT held that in cases such as the present where a state of undress was inevitably incidental to the work, the "genuine occupational qualification" exception of preserving decency applied. This was not limited only to cases where the actual work was done in a state of undress.

2. Work outside Great Britain

Haughton v *Olau Lines (UK) Ltd* (1986)

Claims for sex discrimination are excluded if employment is not at an establishment in Great Britain. This includes a person whose work is done wholly or mainly outside Great Britain such as on a cross-channel ferry.

Mrs Haughton's employment was terminated after she fell out with the purser on the cross-channel ferry where she worked. She brought a claim for compensation claiming that she had been unlawfully discriminated against.

The employer claimed that as her work was not at an establishment in Great Britain the tribunal had no jurisdiction to hear the claim. This was held to be the case. Her claim was excluded as her employment was wholly or mainly outside Great Britain.

3. Doctor not appointed as general practitioner: whether "employment"; statutory procedure

Ealing, Hammersmith and Hounslow Family Health Services Authority v *Shukla* (1993)

For the purposes of the Sex Discrimination Act 1975, the appointment of a doctor as a general practitioner does not constitute "employment".

When the medical practices committee of the British Medical Association, acting on the recommendations of the respondent family health services authority, failed to appoint S, a doctor, as a general practitioner to a practice where he had been employed as an assistant and locum, he complained that he had been discriminated against because of his sex. The industrial tribunal, on a preliminary issue as to jurisdiction, held that the appointment of a general practitioner was "employment" as it was defined by section 82(1) of the Act and therefore a complaint could be brought under section 6(10)(a). Section 82(1) provides that "employment" means employment under a contract of service or apprenticeship or a contract personally to execute any work or labour. The family health services authority appealed.

The appeal was allowed. The appointment of a general practitioner did not constitute "employment" as it was defined by section 82(1) for the purposes of section 6(1)(a). It was not a "contract personally to execute any work of labour". The arrangements made to determine who should be offered the position of general practitioner were not made by the family health services authority within the meaning of section 6(1)(a), but were a fixed statutory procedure. The industrial tribunal therefore had no jurisdiction to hear the complaint.

Key problem areas

- Meaning of "detriment" for purposes of the 1975 Act
- Sexual harassment, *i.e.* meaning; amount of compensation; "detriment"; and burden of proof
- Meaning of "justification" as a defence
- Age requirements: whether discriminatory
- "Requirement or condition": problems of definition
- Redundancy selection: sex discrimination implications
- Reasonableness of requirements or conditions
- Insistence by employer on full-time working
- Constructive dismissal: adverse treatment on grounds of sex
- Unfair dismissal: continuity of employment
- Meaning of "less favourable treatment"
- Genuine occupational qualification: preservation of decency
- Work outside Great Britain
- Meaning of "employment" for purposes of the 1975 Act

CHAPTER 3

Pregnancy

Pregnancy-related absence from work: comparison with male employee absent through long-term illness

Pregnancy dismissal

1. Misconduct whilst pregnant: comparison with male incapacitated by illness; no reference to question of misconduct; whether tribunal erred in law
2. Dismissal due to absence through sickness: whether positive evidence of employer's treatment of male employee necessary
3. Whether tribunal erred in basing decision on comparable situation involving man
4. Assessment of compensation
5. Compulsory discharge; compensation; whether appropriate basis of assessment used
6. Unmarried school matron dismissed on pregnancy: whether unlawful sex discrimination

Key problem areas

CHAPTER 3

Pregnancy

Pregnancy-related absence from work: comparison with male employee absent through long-term illness

Brown v *Rentokil* (1992)
After having been absent on sick leave for more than 26 weeks, B was dismissed. This accorded with R's policy. She had been absent due to several pregnancy-related causes.

The tribunal found that she had been treated in the same way as a male employee who had been absent due to long-term illness. Her claim of sex discrimination was dismissed.

The EAT dismissed her appeal. B had failed to prove that she had been treated less favourably than a man in comparable circumstances. She had therefore not been subject to sex discrimination. This accorded with the decision in *Webb* v *EMO Air Cargo (UK)* rather than that taken in *James* v *Eastleigh BC* where it was proved that the man and the woman had been treated differently.

Pregnancy dismissal

1. Misconduct whilst pregnant: comparison with male incapacitated by illness; no reference to question of misconduct: whether tribunal erred in law

Shomer v *B&R Residential Lettings* (1992)
S was dismissed allegedly on grounds of misconduct whilst she was pregnant. She complained of sex discrimination. It was found by the tribunal that a hypothetical male employee who was incapacitated by illness would not have been dismissed in the same circumstances. It upheld her complaint by a majority. However, compensation was reduced by one-third on the ground of contributory fault. The employer appealed to the EAT.

This appeal was allowed and S appealed to the Court of Appeal. S's appeal was dismissed. It was found that the majority of the tribunal had made an error in finding that S had been subject to sex discrimination whilst pregnant.

The tribunal had misdirected itself in comparing her with a hypothetical male who was incapacitated by an illness. She had committed an act of serious misconduct. Under the tests laid down by *Webb* v *EMO Air Cargo (UK)* which entitled the tribunal to consider whether a man would have been dismissed in comparable circumstances, all relevant circumstances must be taken into account. This is covered by section 5(3) of the 1975 Act. The tribunal had not taken into account the question of the misconduct of the hypothetical man and had therefore erred in law.

2. Dismissal due to absence through sickness: whether positive evidence of employer's treatment of male employee necessary

East Berkshire Health Authority v *Matadeen* (1992)

Section 1(1)(a) of the 1975 Act must of necessity involve a hypothesis as to how a man would be treated in similar circumstances. P was a cook at a private hospital. When she became pregnant she informed her employer. She failed to attend work on a number of days and was dismissed by a letter which stated that she had repudiated the terms of her contract in that she had missed work without telling them the reason. P claimed unlawful discrimination on the ground of sex under sections 1(1)(a) and 6(2)(b) of the Act.

It was found by the tribunal that part of the reason for the dismissal was P's pregnancy. The only evidence which the employer had provided to show how a man with a similar disability would be treated was a statement from the managing director that it would have treated a man with a known sickness disability, absent from work without explanation, in the same way. This was not accepted by the tribunal which held that P had been unlawfully discriminated against because of her sex. The employers' appeal was dismissed by the EAT:

- A hypothesis was necessarily involved in the wording of section 1(1)(a) whereby a person discriminates against a woman if she is treated less favourably than he "treats or would treat a man".
- It was unrealistic to regard the Act as requiring positive evidence about how a man with a comparable disability had been treated in the past in relation to a similar absence.
- The tribunal had been entitled to infer that a man with a known sickness disability would not have been dismissed in similar circumstances after considering all the evidence.

3. Whether tribunal erred in basing decision on comparable situation involving man

Dixon v *Rees*; *Hopkins* v *Shepherd and Partners* (1993)

After D became pregnant she was dismissed from her job, due, her employer said, to her insubordination. The tribunal dismissed her claim of sex discrimination. It found that she was dismissed because her employer had found a replacement for her and there was no evidence to show that a man would have been treated any differently. She had not been dismissed purely as a result of her pregnancy.

H, a veterinary nurse, was dismissed when she became pregnant because it would no longer be safe for her to continue because of the nature of her work.

D and H both appealed. They held that the comparative test was no longer valid after the decisions in *Webb* v *EMO Air Cargo (UK)* and *Dekker* v *Stichting Vormingscentrum voor Jonge Volwassenen Plus*. The appeals were dismissed by the EAT which held that it was up to the tribunal to consider how a man would have been treated in comparable circumstances when an employee had been dismissed because of the consequences rather than the fact of pregnancy. Therefore the tribunal had not erred in basing its decision on how a man would have been treated by the employers in similar circumstances.

4. Assessment of compensation

Ministry of Defence v *Cannock* (1994)

Successful unfair dismissal claims were brought by approximately 4,000 women following the MOD's concession that its former practice of dismissing pregnant women was in contravention of the EC Equal Treatment Directive and therefore unlawful. Guidelines in relation to compensation in seven selected cases which raised contentious issues were sought and the MOD appealed to the EAT.

The EAT held that the applicants should be put in the financial positions in which they would have been but for the MoD's unlawful conduct in dismissing them, in order to calculate the correct measure of damages for claims brought under the Directive. The EAT made the following statements:

- It had been correctly held by the tribunal that an applicant's failure to apply to rejoin the service related to mitigation rather than causation.

- Loss of congenial employment could be covered by an award for injury to feelings.
- There was no separate head of damage for loss of career prospects.
- Loss of pension benefits could be awarded for periods prior to the European Court's decision in *Barber*.
- The child-care costs which the applicants would have incurred on their return to work should be offset against damages.
- The period over which interest was awarded was within the discretion of the tribunal. Interest in respect of pension losses could not be awarded by the tribunal. The tribunal had not erred in awarding interest on damages for injury to feelings.

The tribunal must assess the following factors in assessing compensation for loss of earnings:

- The chances that the applicant would have returned to work if given the opportunity.
- The chances of the applicant being in a position to return to work if the opportunity was given.
- The length of service hypothetically lost.
- The chances of promotion.
- The effect of other contingencies such as the birth of subsequent children.

The EAT considered that some of the large awards were wholly unjustified in the present cases. They were manifestly excessive, wrong in principle and out of proportion.

5. Compulsory discharge; compensation; whether appropriate basis of assessment used

Ministry of Defence v Sullivan (1994)
An industrial tribunal had to determine what loss had flowed from the unlawful act of discrimination and although it was not obliged to adopt a comparator approach, it was entitled to when assessing compensation for sex discrimination.

A dental nurse with the Royal Navy was told, on becoming pregnant, that she must apply for a compulsory discharge. Seven years after her discharge she was awarded compensation by an industrial tribunal for breach of article 2 of EC Directive 76/207 because she had been discriminated against by reason of her sex.

The award was based on comparison with a man suffering from an injury which would incapacitate him for nine months and comprised loss of earnings up to confinement and six months loss of earnings after confinement. She was also awarded £750 for injury to her feelings.

The MOD's appeal was dismissed. It was held by the EAT that the tribunal was entitled, although not obliged, to adopt a comparator approach when assessing compensation to determine what loss flowed from the unlawful act of discrimination. The tribunal had erred in law in assessing compensation on the basis of an injured man resuming his duties after nine months' incapacity. Since the woman was entitled to compensation for a period after the birth in which she was not obliged to mitigate her loss by seeking new employment and since six months was an appropriate period for such a decision, the tribunal had reached the right result. The £750 awarded for injury to feelings was justified.

6. Unmarried school matron dismissed on pregnancy: whether unlawful sex discrimination

Berrisford v *Woodard Schools (Midland Division)* (1991)

An unmarried school matron, B, was dismissed when she became pregnant and did not intend to get married. In evidence the employer stated that it was not the pregnancy that was the reason for her dismissal. In similar matters relating to moral issues, male members of staff had been treated in a similar manner. The tribunal dismissed her complaint of sex discrimination.

B's appeal was dismissed by the EAT. It was found that she had not been discriminated against on the grounds of sex contrary to sections 1(1)(a) and 6(2)(b) of the 1975 Act.

- The tribunal was correct in finding that it was not because of her pregnancy that she had been dismissed.
- She had been dismissed because her employer considered that her conduct was not a suitable example to the school pupils and there was evidence to show that male employees were treated comparably in respect to similar moral issues.
- Just because a man could not become pregnant, it did not mean that sex discrimination was naturally involved in a dismissal because it involved pregnancy.

Key problem areas

- Relationship between misconduct and pregnancy
- Problems of gender comparison
- Relationship between sickness and pregnancy
- Compensation levels
- Unmarried employees: moral issues

CHAPTER 4

Retirement

Whether EC law should be applied

Different age for different categories of workers: whether based on sex: whether direct or indirect discrimination

Applicability of EC Directive: whether employer a commercial undertaking

Equal Treatment Directive: "organs of the State"; whether body providing public service within scope of Directive

Employment policy: persons retired early not employed: higher proportion of men than women in receipt of occupational pensions: whether indirect discrimination: whether policy justifiable

Key problem areas

CHAPTER 4

Retirement

Whether EC law should be applied

Porter v *Cannon Hygiene* (1993)

When P was dismissed at the age of 60 she brought a claim of sex discrimination on the basis that a man would not be required to retire until he was 65 years of age. Since her dismissal had occurred before the exclusion relating to discriminatory retirement contained in article 8(4) of the Sex Discrimination (Northern Ireland) Order 1976 was removed to comply with article 5(1) of the EC Equal Treatment Directive, her claim was dismissed.

P contended that the tribunal had erred in law in its construction of *Finnegan* v *Clowney Youth Training Programme* [1990] and *Duke* v *GEC Reliance (formerly Reliance Systems)* [1988] which it had followed. She therefore appealed.

The appeal was dismissed. The tribunal had been correct in applying the principles in *Finnegan* to dismiss P's claim. It was not the duty of a national court to interpret domestic law so as not to conflict with EC law.

The exclusion formerly contained in domestic law had only one possible construction in the present case. It was only where there was more than one possible construction of national law that the court should prefer the construction which accorded with EC law rather than that which did not.

Different age for different categories of workers: whether based on sex: whether direct or indirect discrimination

Bullock v *Alice Ottley School* (1992)

B was dismissed when she reached the school's retirement age of 60 for administrative and domestic staff. She brought a claim of sex discrimination, claiming that male colleagues were allowed to work until the age of 65.

It was contended by the school that a common retirement age for groups of staff had been established, regardless of sex. This was 60 for teaching, administrative and domestic staff and 65 for gardeners and maintenance staff.

B's complaint was dismissed by the tribunal which found that provided they were irrespective of sex it was not discriminatory to have different retirement ages for employees in different groups. B appealed to the EAT.

Her appeal was allowed as it was held that retiring ages must be the same for all employees. The school appealed. This appeal was allowed and the tribunal's decision restored. It was held that the EAT was in error to find that the school had discriminated against B on grounds of her sex. Provided that there was no direct or indirect discrimination based on gender, the 1975 Act did not prevent an employer from having different retirement ages for employees engaged in different jobs. Since it was difficult to recruit staff for the positions of gardeners and maintenance men, it was necessary to retain them for as long as possible and the school had therefore shown there was a real and genuine need for a later retirement age for employees in these jobs.

The EAT's conclusion that all employees of the same employer should have the same retirement age was rejected.

Applicability of EC Directive: whether employer a commercial undertaking

Doughty v *Rolls Royce* (1992)
D retired at the age of 60. Her employer had a policy of compulsory retirement for men at 65 years of age and for women at 60 years of age. D claimed unlawful discrimination contrary to the EC Equal Treatment Directive.

The industrial tribunal held that, as the state was her employer's sole shareholder at the relevant time, it had the power to require the directors to alter contracts of employment so that they complied with the Directive. Therefore under EC law D was entitled to rely directly on the Directive to bring her complaint. The employer's appeal was allowed by the EAT on the basis that since it was not an agent of the state carrying out a state function then it was not a body against which the provisions of the Directive were directly enforceable.

D appealed. She argued that, following the decision in *Foster* v *British*

Gas (below) the only relevant test was whether the employer was under the control of the state. The appeal was dismissed. The EAT had been correct to conclude that the provisions of the Directive were not directly enforceable by D against the employer.

There were several criteria for determining whether the provisions of the Directive were directly enforceable against a particular body. The element of control was only one of these. In *Foster* there were three criteria established for determining the status of a body, *i.e.* whether:

- it was "made responsible, pursuant to a measure adopted by the state, for providing a public service"
- the "service" it provided was at the material time "under the control of the state"
- it possessed, or claimed to exercise, any "special powers".

D could not seek direct reliance upon the provisions of the Directive as in the present case: neither the first nor the third requirement were met.

Equal Treatment Directive: "organs of the State"; whether body providing public service within scope of Directive

Foster v British Gas (1988)

F and others worked for British Gas. They were dismissed in 1985 and 1986 when they reached the company's compulsory retirement age for women. They claimed that, according to EC law, they had been unlawfully discriminated against.

At that time the Sex Discrimination Act 1986, which made discriminatory retirement ages unlawful, was not yet in force and British Gas had not yet been privatised. The application was dismissed by the tribunal on the grounds that article 5 of the EC Equal Treatment Directive only referred to "organs of the State"; this did not include British Gas. Appeals were dismissed by both the EAT and the Court of Appeal. The case was referred to the European Court by the House of Lords for a preliminary ruling on the question of whether the British Gas Corporation was at the material time a body of such type that F and others were entitled to rely upon the Equal Treatment Directive in the English courts and to claim damages on the ground that its retirement policy was contrary to the Directive.

Article 5(1) could be relied on against a body, whatever its legal form, which had been made responsible for providing a public service under the control of the state and had for that purpose special powers beyond those which resulted from the normal rules applicable in relations between individuals. It was unconditional and sufficiently precise to be applied by national courts and to be relied on by an individual. A member state would not be entitled to rely upon its own failure to implement a directive.

Employment policy: persons retired early not employed: higher proportion of men than women in receipt of occupational pensions: whether indirect discrimination: whether policy justifiable

Greater Manchester Police Authority v *LEA* (1990)

L had taken compulsory medical retirement and was in receipt of an occupational pension. He was rejected for employment by the authority because it had a policy of not employing those who had been retired early from other employment in order to take account of the needs of the unemployed.

Since a higher proportion of men than women in the economically active proportion of the population were in receipt of occupational pensions, L claimed that he had suffered indirect sex discrimination. His claim was upheld by the tribunal. The authority appealed. The appeal was dismissed.

- The tribunal had been correct to accept that the economically active population was the appropriate pool to consider when deciding who could comply with the authority's policy.
- As the figures were 99.4% for women and 95.3% for men, then it was a "considerably smaller" proportion of men who could comply with the policy and the tribunal had been correct in so finding.
- The tribunal had also been correct in finding that the authority had failed to show that its policy was justifiable.

Key problem areas

- EC law implications (see Chapter 7 for summaries of main EC cases)
- Different categories of worker: differing retirement ages
- Meaning of commercial undertaking
- Organs of the state: British Gas
- Employment policy in relation to retirement ages: whether justifiable

Equal Pay

Equal Pay Act 1970

Material factor defence

1. Comparator paid more by mistake: whether employer could rely on mistake
2. Work of equal value: comparators at other establishments; whether common terms and conditions
3. Like work: male instructor paid more than female: error as to qualifications: whether sufficient to show no intention to discriminate
4. Hours of work: whether employer obliged to prove objective justification for difference in pay
5. Whether burden of proof entirely on employer
6. Details of salary histories of comparators provided: whether further and better particulars to be ordered

Job evaluation study carried out in great Britain: whether applicable to Northern Ireland

Redundancy: whether EC law directly enforceable

Pensions

1. Occupational pension scheme: deduction of state pension: whether equality of pay with male comparator: whether breach of EC law
2. Whether pension payments are "pay" under EC law: whether EC law applies

Salary grading provisions; whether applicant's work rated as equivalent

Key problem areas

CHAPTER 5

Equal Pay

Equal Pay Act 1970

The Act requires equal terms and conditions of employment for men and women in the same employment in two situations.

1. When employed on "like work", which means work of the same or a broadly similar nature.
2. When employed on work rated as equivalent under a job evaluation study.

Material factor defence

I. Comparator paid more by mistake; whether employer could rely on mistake

Yorkshire Blood Transfusion Service v *Plaskitt* (1994)
An employer's mistake could be relied on as a material factor, which was not the difference in sex, in defence of an equal pay claim.

A was employed as a medical laboratory scientific officer, Grade 1, at a blood transfusion centre which operated under the NHS. She was paid under Whatley Council Rules and on point 19 of the relevant pay scale. She claimed equality of pay with a male comparator. He was also a scientific officer Grade 1 but he had previously been in different employment and his salary had been maintained at point 23 of the pay scale when he gained his current employment.

It was held by the tribunal that the employers were in breach of section 1(2)(a) of the Equal Pay Act 1970. The employer appealed.

The appeal was allowed. When seeking to establish a genuine material factor defence under section 1(3) of the 1970 Act it was not necessary for an employer to provide objectively justified grounds for the difference in pay. The employer's mistake in employing the comparator at the wrong salary rather than any difference of sex within the meaning of section 1(3) was the cause of the difference in pay.

2. Work of equal value: comparators at other establishments; whether common terms and conditions

British Coal Corp. v *Smith* (1993)

There must be common terms and conditions of employment when comparing a member of the applicant's class at her workplace with a member of the comparator's class at his in order to make a comparison under section 1(2)(c) of the 1970 Act.

S and A were female canteen workers and cleaners who were employed by one employer at 47 establishments. They sought equality of pay with a number of male comparators who were surface mineworkers or clerical workers employed by the same employer at different establishments. They stated that they were doing work of equal value within section 1(2)(c). As preliminary issues, it was considered by an industrial tribunal whether S and A were in the "same employment" as the comparators pursuant to section 1(6) of the 1970 Act and whether it had been established by the employer that the variation in pay was due to a material factor other than sex pursuant to section 1(3), this being collective agreements entered into without reference to sex.

The tribunal agreed that cleaners and clerical staff had common terms and conditions of employment at their different establishments and were therefore to be treated as in the same employment. It found also that canteen workers and mineworkers had common terms and conditions and were to be treated as in the same employment. Therefore, the tribunal found that S and A were to be treated as in the "same employment" as their named comparators within section 6.

As it found that the employer had failed to show that the variation in pay was genuinely due to a material factor which was not the difference of sex within the meaning of section 1(3), the tribunal referred the claims for independent expert assessment. The employer appealed.

The appeal was allowed in part. Section 1(6) requires that common terms and conditions must be observed in each establishment where a comparison was made under section 1(2)(c) of a member of S and A's class at their establishment with a member of the comparator's class at his. On the evidence, canteen workers and mineworkers were entitled to such common terms and conditions. The tribunal had been in error in its approach to the issues raised by section 1(3). The tribunal's findings were only sufficient to establish discrimination in relation to some workers, such as in relation to the comparison between canteen workers and mineworkers where the findings did establish indirect discrimination. They were insufficient to establish discrimination in relation to other workers. However, since the condition for receiving concessionary coal or a bonus for work at the coal face was a condition with which women could not comply, and since the employer had failed to justify that condition, the defence under section 1(3) failed in that respect.

3. Like work: male instructor paid more than female: error as to qualifications: whether sufficient to show no intention to discriminate

McPherson v Rathgael Centre for Children and Young People and Northern Ireland Office (Training School Branch) (1991)
M was an outdoor pursuits instructor. On the ground that she was paid less than a male instructor, she brought an equal pay claim. It had been believed when his employment commenced that he had a teaching qualification and therefore he was paid on a higher scale.

It was later found that his qualifications did not qualify him for the higher scale. The employer's defence was that M was paid on the right scale and that the male instructor was being paid on the wrong scale due to an error. The fact that he was a man was purely coincidental.

M's appeal was allowed. The tribunal had been in error to find that there was a genuine material difference between M and the male instructor other than sex.. It was not sufficient for an employer to show there was no intention to discriminate, which could only succeed in a defence to an equal pay claim if it could establish that there were objectively justifiable grounds for the variation in levels of pay.

4. Hours of work: whether employer obliged to prove objective justification for difference in pay

Calder and Cizakowsky v Rowntree Mackintosh Confectionery (1992)
A1 and A2 worked from 5.30 pm to 10.30 pm. They brought equal pay claims and compared their work with a male comparator who received a "shift premium" for working rotating shifts. Female employees who also worked on rotating shifts also received a "shift premium".

The employer's defence under section 1(3) of the 1970 Act was that the differential in pay was due to the inconvenience of working rotating shifts and the unsociable hours involved. This was upheld by the tribunal.

A1 and A2 appealed. They argued that the employer was required to show "objective justification" for the difference in pay and that they too worked unsociable hours. The appeal was dismissed on the following grounds:

- The employer had established at least one material factor which was capable of justifying the difference on its own.
- Unless direct discrimination was alleged it was not necessary for the employer to prove objective justification for the difference.
- The tribunal had been correct in dismissing the claim on the basis of its finding that the difference in pay was due to the factors of inconvenience of rotating shifts and unsociable hours, rather than to the difference of sex, and was not obliged to apportion the difference in pay between the two factors.

5. Whether burden of proof entirely on employer

Financial Times v *Byrne (No 2)* (1992)

It was claimed by female employees that they were employed on like work or work of equal value with a range of male comparators. The employer claimed that the differences in pay were due to a number of material factors under section 1(3) of the 1970 Act.

As a preliminary point, the employees sought a breakdown of their salaries and those of the comparators. Such an order was refused by the industrial tribunal. The tribunal also held that the burden of proof was entirely on the employer in respect of a defence under section 3(1).

The employer's appeal against the tribunal's refusal to grant an order in respect of the breakdown was dismissed. The tribunal had found correctly that the employer was required unambiguously by section 3(1) to prove that the variations were due to a material factor and that they were not due to a difference in sex.

6. Details of salary histories of comparators provided: whether further and better particulars to be ordered

Byrne v *Financial Times* (1991)

It was claimed by the 11 applicants that they performed like work or work of equal value to a range of comparators. The employer claimed it had a defence under section 1(3) of the 1970 Act as the differences in pay were justified on grounds of a number of factors which were not related to sex. Details of the salary histories of the comparators were provided by the employer but the applicants sought further and better particulars in respect of the breakdown and attribution of specific sums to the alleged different factors. When the tribunal refused their application the applicants appealed.

The appeal was dismissed. The tribunal had been correct to refuse to order further particulars of a breakdown of the comparators' salaries and an allocation of the salaries to various factors. Such a breakdown was subjective rather than objective and therefore it was in reality impossible to provide. The tribunal had properly applied the principles relating to the order of particulars which included the following:

- that the parties should not be taken by surprise at the last minute;
- that particulars should only be ordered when necessary to do justice or to avoid adjournment;
- that the order should not be oppressive;
- that the particulars were for the purposes of identifying issues and not for producing evidence.

Job evaluation study carried out in Great Britain: whether applicable to Northern Ireland

McAuley v *Eastern Health and Social Services Board* (1991)

M and four others were employed as domestic assistants at the Royal Victoria Hospital in Belfast. They brought an equal value complaint comparing their work to that of a male groundsman and a male domestic porter.

The employer's argument, under section 1(6) of the Northern Ireland Equal Pay Act 1970, was that it had relied upon a job evaluation study which was carried out in Great Britain in respect of health service and ancillary workers. It stated that section 1(6) of the Northern Ireland Act was exactly the same as section 1(5) of the British Equal Pay Act 1970 and argued that the British study applied equally to the same type of workers in Northern Ireland.

The employer's argument was rejected by the tribunal. It found that there was no evidence that the study carried out in Great Britain should apply to Northern Ireland.

The employer's appeal was dismissed. The tribunal had been correct in its decision that the work of M and the four others could not be regarded as having been given different values under a job evaluation study carried out in Great Britain. Their claims could not, therefore, be precluded on these grounds.

Redundancy: whether EC law directly enforceable

McKechnie v *UBM Building Supplies (Southern)* (1991)
Prior to implementation of the provisions of the Employment Act 1989, M was made redundant at the age of 61. She was therefore not entitled to a statutory redundancy payment or to a payment under the employer's voluntary scheme.

She claimed that she was entitled to the same treatment as a man of identical age under the provisions of article 119 of the EEC Treaty. The tribunal applied the decision in *Burton* v *British Railways Board* and dismissed her claim. The decision was issued before the decision in *Barber* v *Guardian Royal Exchange*.

M's appeal was allowed. The tribunal was in error to hold that she was not entitled to be treated in the same way as a man of the same age. Directly enforceable rights by individuals against employers had been conferred by article 119. It had been wrong to apply the decision in *Burton* rather than the decision in *Barber*, which made it clear that statutory and ex gratia redundancy payments came properly within the definition of "pay" in article 119.

Pensions

1. Occupational pension scheme: deduction of state pension: whether equality of pay with male comparator: whether breach of EC law

Roberts v *Birds Eye Wall's* (1992)
At the age of 57, R retired on grounds of ill health. She received from her employer's superannuation scheme an annual pension and a further sum from a discretionary scheme. This scheme was subject to bridging conditions on the basis that after she received her state pension when she was 60 her entitlement to a sum from the scheme would be reduced.

R claimed that the bridging provisions were contrary to article 119 of the EEC Treaty. Her claim was rejected by the tribunal. She appealed to the EAT after the decision in *Barber* v *Guardian Royal Exchange Assurance Group*.

The EAT held that the employer would be depriving her of her entitlement to the same "pay" as her male comparators if it deducted the state pension from her occupational pension. The employer appealed to the Court of Appeal. The decision of that court was as follows:

"In order to determine whether Article 119 prohibits an employer who operates a discretionary occupational pension scheme from making a deduction from a woman's pension from the age of 60, by reason of her entitlement to a state pension, but who makes no such deduction from a man's pension, since he would not be entitled to receive a state pension until the age of 65, the case would be referred to the European Court of Justice."

It would be ironic if the effect of applying article 119 were to counteract the provisions of the scheme which existed so that both men and women would receive the same aggregate sum from state and occupational pension at all times and in order to overcome the disparity which currently existed in English law. If the decision in *Barber* was applied this was the conclusion it led to unless objectively justified criteria were applied to distinguish the case. The European Court of Justice was the body to properly consider this.

2. Whether pension payments are "pay" under EC law: whether EC law applies

Griffin v *London Pension Fund Authority* (1993)

When G retired at the age of 44 due to ill health she received a reduced pension. When she reached the age of 60 it was reduced further as she then became entitled to a state pension. G claimed that if she had been a man then her pension would not have been reduced further until she reached the age of 65 and therefore this was in breach of article 119 of the EEC Treaty and the Equal Pay Directive.

Her complaint was dismissed by the tribunal on the grounds that the pension payments were social security payments rather than "pay". G appealed. The appeal was dismissed.

- The tribunal had been correct to find that the pension payments were not "pay" in accordance with the decision in *Barber*.
- There was a difference between payments made under a statutory social security scheme, which were not "pay", and those made under a contracted-out private scheme, which were "pay".
- The scheme in this instance was statutory and applied to all local government workers.
- Since G's pension position had crystallised before the EC Treaty was given legal effect in the United Kingdom, she could not in any event rely on EC law.

Salary grading provisions; whether applicant's work rated as equivalent

Springboard Sunderland Trust v *Robson* (1992)

R, after an appeal, had been awarded 410 points under a job evaluation scheme by which Springboard Sunderland Trust, her employer, determined pay. She claimed she was entitled to pay equal to a male comparator whose job had been awarded 428 points. Under the scheme jobs with between 410 and 449 points would be at salary grade 4. R was paid at salary grade 3. Her claim was upheld by the industrial tribunal, although the chairman dissented on the grounds that the value of points awarded should be equal to the male comparator, not the conversion to a salary grade.

The employer's appeal was dismissed. The decision of the majority of the industrial tribunal was correct. Notwithstanding the disparity in points the work was of equal value within the provisions of section 1(5) of the 1970 Act as a result of the salary grading provisions. In assessing the value of work regard must be taken of the full results of a job grading scheme.

Key problem areas

- Material factor defence: effect of mistake; comparison with other establishments; common terms and conditions; burden of proof – objective justification; further and better particulars
- Job evaluation study: Northern Ireland
- Redundancy: effect of EC law
- Occupational pensions: effect of EC law
- Meaning of "pay": occupational pensions
- Salary grading

Industrial Tribunal Practice and Procedure

Complaints

EAT: jurisdiction: new point raised: further evidence required: whether to be heard by tribunal

Time limits

1. Whether second respondent can be added outside time limit
2. Redundancy payments: women treated less favourably than men: effect of EC law
3. Company take-over: decision not to employ male salesmen: decision made known on completion of take-over: whether complaints made in time

Industrial tribunal

1. Procedure: discovery of documents
2. Jurisdiction: agreement precluding complaints: claim under EC law
3. Complaint of sex discrimination made by woman assistant chief constable: discovery and inspection: whether public interest immunity: whether bias: whether tribunal members to be selected for specialist knowledge
4. Sex discrimination hearing postponed pending determination of relevant cases: restoration of application sought four years after decisions given: whether justifiable
5. Promotion whether tribunal's decision should be interfered with

Damages and compensation

1. Damages: discrimination on grounds of sex and race: local authority post at college: industrial tribunal's award of damages: whether appropriate to include exemplary damages
2. Amount of compensation in claim of sex discrimination

Key problem areas

CHAPTER 6

Industrial Tribunal Practice and Procedure

Complaints

Complaints of sex discrimination under the 1975 Act, where they relate to employment matters, must be brought before an industrial tribunal within three months of the act complained of. In other areas, action is taken through the county court.

EAT: jurisdiction: new point raised: further evidence required: whether to be heard by tribunal

Barber v *Thames Television* (1991)

The EAT had to decide whether justice required that a new point should be taken into account where an issue arose as to how far the new point, which raised a question of jurisdiction, could be considered by it, notwithstanding that further evidence would be required.

In order to provide for the progressive reduction of retirement ages B's employer altered its pension scheme. B had elected to retire at 65 years of age but he was notified that in accordance with the scheme he would have to retire at 64 years of age. He was dismissed on his 64th birthday. He complained of unfair dismissal. As a preliminary issue the industrial tribunal considered whether there was a normal retiring age for an employee in his position within the meaning of section 64(1)(b) of the Employment Protection (Consolidation) Act 1978. He would be deprived of his normal right to bring a complaint if he had reached this age. The tribunal found that prior to 1987 there was no normal retiring age but after that date all employees knew the date when they would be compelled to retire. As B had reached his normal retiring age at 64 the tribunal had no jurisdiction to hear the complaint. When B appealed the employer sought leave to amend its notice so as to raise the point that the normal retiring age was 60.

B's appeal was allowed. All those holding the same position as B and notified as he was, in October 1987, of the transitional provisions regarding retiring ages had been selected as a group by the employer. It was only by the employer's employment policy that such a group could by distinguished and not by the terms and conditions of employment as required by the definition of "position" in section 153(1) of the 1978 Act. The tribunal had therefore been in error in identifying those to whom a normal retiring age would be applied. The correct group was all the senior supervisors of equal status to B whether or not they were subject to the transitional provisions.

Section 64(1)(b) did not apply as a number of these had a retirement age of 60 whilst others retired according to the transitional provisions. The tribunal therefore had jurisdiction to hear the complaint. The EAT had to decide whether on balance justice required that a new point be heard if a party to an appeal contended that by calling further evidence it could be shown that the case fell outside the tribunal's jurisdiction. The position was less straightforward if what was relied on was a chance of establishing a lack of jurisdiction by calling fresh evidence that had always been available than if it appeared that on existing evidence the decision appealed from was a nullity. In the latter case that would be an overwhelming consideration. The employer's application for leave to amend was refused as the EAT did not consider it just for the employer to try to persuade the tribunal that B was disqualified under section 64(1)(b) by adducing evidence that skilled advisers had chosen not to adduce.

Time limits

1. Whether second respondent can be added outside time limit

Gillick v *BP Chemicals* (1993)
A claim of sex discrimination against the company which had contracted her services out to BP Chemicals, relating to acts committed between May 1988 and September 1991, was brought by G in October 1991. Upon G's application in February 1992 it was ordered by the tribunal that BP Chemicals be joined as a respondent. When it was held at a preliminary hearing that the claim against BP Chemicals was out of time, G appealed.

The appeal was allowed. In the case of the addition or substitution of a respondent there was no time limit as such. Regardless of whether the respective companies were associated companies or not, it was a matter of discretion for the tribunal on the facts of each case.

2. Redundancy payments: women treated less favourably than men: effect of EC law

Rankin v *British Coal Corpn* (1993)

When R was made redundant in March 1987 she did not receive redundancy payment as she was 61 years old, although men were entitled to receive payments up to the age of 65. This was under the provisions of the Employment Protection (Consolidation) Act 1978 which was in force at that time. The difference in treatment was removed by the Employment Act 1989, although not retrospectively, with effect from January 1990. The European Court of Justice held that redundancy payments fall within the scope of "pay" in article 119 of the EEC Treaty in May 1990. R made a claim that she was entitled to a redundancy payment under article 119 in April 1990. Her application was dismissed by the tribunal on the ground that it was out of time.

R's appeal was allowed. Since R's claim was brought under article 119 the tribunal had erred in basing its decision on the provisions relating to the time limits in section 101 of the 1978 Act. Such limits as are considered to be reasonable should be applied by the national courts, although there are no specified time limits for claims under article 119. R's claim was considered to be in time as it was made within three months of amending legislation.

3. Company take-over: decision not to employ male salesmen: decision made known on completion of take-over: whether complaints made in time

Swithland Motors v *Clarke* (1994)

It was not possible to commit the unlawful act of sex discrimination by omitting to offer employment contrary to section 6(1)(c) of the 1975 Act until the employer was in a position to offer such employment.

A company (SM) was negotiating with receivers to buy the assets of company C. A were employed by company C. They were interviewed by SM. A were informed by SM the day after the take-over was signed that they were being dismissed by C and not being taken on by SM. Complaints of sex discrimination under section 6(1)(c) were brought by A who alleged that SM had a policy of only recruiting female sales staff. It was held by the industrial tribunal that in three cases the decision not to employ A had been taken on the day of the interview in three cases and the day after in the fourth case; therefore they were out of time under section 76(1). It was, however, just and equitable to consider them pursuant to section 76(6).

The appeal by SM was dismissed by the EAT which held that the unlawful act of sex discrimination by omitting to offer employment contrary to section 6(1)(c) could not be committed until the alleged discriminator was in a position to offer such employment. Therefore the complaints were in time as SM was not in a position to offer employment until completion of the take-over.

Industrial tribunal

1. Procedure: discovery of documents

Nassé v *Science Research Council* (1979)
The industrial tribunal must inspect the documents if the employee asks for disclosure of documents which the employer regards as confidential. If it finds that it is in the interests of justice or of saving costs it can only then order disclosure.

Mrs Nasse claimed sex discrimination when she was effectively barred from promotion by not being asked to attend a promotion interview. She asked for access to confidential reports made on two of her colleagues who were asked to attend an interview but her employer refused. Eventually the case came before the House of Lords.

Industrial tribunals are governed by rule 2(2) of the County Court Rules and have the same jurisdiction over discovery of documents as the county courts. Therefore "discovery shall not be ordered if the court is of the opinion that it is not necessary either for disposing fairly of the proceedings or for saving costs." A tribunal must order disclosure if it forms the view that it is necessary for a fair disposal of the case and there is no rule of privilege on confidential documents, or presumption against disclosure. The case was remitted to the industrial tribunal.

2. Jurisdiction: agreement precluding complaints: claim under EC law

Livingstone v *Hepworth Refractories* (1992)
L's employment was terminated. In April 1990 he signed a form COT3 whereby he agreed to accept a sum in full and final settlement of all claims "except for any benefits due to him under the rules of the company's pension scheme". He made a claim of sex discrimination under the provisions of the 1975 Act and EC law after the decision in *Barber* v

Guardian Royal Exchange Assurance Group. The case was dismissed by the tribunal. It was held that it had no jurisdiction because of the COT3 agreement.

L's appeal was allowed by the EAT. The tribunal had been in error in finding that it had no jurisdiction. Unless it expressly stated so a COT3 agreement drawn up under the provisions of the Employment Protection (Consolidation) Act 1978 did not cover a claim under either the Sex Discrimination Act 1975 or the Equal Pay Act 1970. Since the courts of member states were required to adopt procedures for the purposes of EC law which were no less favourable than those of domestic law, the provisions of EC law were not excluded. The tribunal should have applied the procedures of the Sex Discrimination Act 1975 to a claim for sex discrimination under EC law.

3. Complaint of sex discrimination made by woman assistant chief constable: discovery and inspection: whether public interest immunity: whether bias: whether tribunal members to be selected for specialist knowledge

Halford v *Sharples* (1992)

A was an assistant chief constable of Merseyside Police. She made a complaint of unlawful sex discrimination contrary to section 1(1)(a) of the Sex Discrimination Act 1975. She said that Rs had failed to support her application for the post of deputy chief constable of Northamptonshire Police, which had been given to a man. She sought disclosure of various documents for which Rs sought public interest immunity. Discovery was granted by the industrial tribunal. An application that one of the lay members on the tribunal, who had been chosen because of his relevant experience, should be replaced due to the fact of his being employed as an equal opportunities officer by another force and had held interviews with members of the force in question was rejected. Interlocutory appeals were made by the chief constable of Merseyside Police to the EAT.

The appeals were allowed. It was held that a party in possession of documents which might be subject to public interest immunity had a duty to raise the issue. It was necessary to find a balance between the public interest in non-disclosure and the interests of justice that documents should be produced. Relevant evidence could only be excluded on clear justification. The residual power to inspect and order disclosure which the EAT retained should be used with extreme care. In a case where the claim was based on the immunity of a class of documents, the respondent should be given an opportunity to appeal before disclosure. If these general principles were applied to the reports on the Merseyside Police Force by Her Majesty's Inspector of Constabulary and to police disciplinary files, which were subject to class privilege, the files should not be disclosed. If the balancing exercise was carried out in the case of files belonging to the Association of Chief Police Officers, documents dealing with positive vetting and the private lives of individual police officers should remain secret. However, production of the officers' personal police records would be ordered to see if on inspection they could be treated as a separate class of which disclosure should be ordered. This was subject to an appeal against the decision that class privilege did not apply to the files as a whole. It was not desirable for lay members to be selected for specialised knowledge. They should be selected at random. They were required to decide facts on the evidence brought before them. If a lay member had made his own investigations it was impossible to know on what basis he had made his decision and a reasonable and disinterested observer might feel that injustice could occur. The lay member would be ordered not to sit further as the tribunal had been wrong in its decision not to replace him.

4. Sex discrimination hearing postponed pending determination of relevant cases: restoration of application sought four years after decisions given: whether justifiable

Sprote v *Commissioner of Police of the Metropolis* (1991)
There was a postponement of the hearing of an originating application in a sex discrimination claim pending the determination of two cases which were considered to be relevant to the claim. The restoration of the application four years after the relevant decisions had been made was not justifiable, as the applicants had stood by in the hope that the law might change in their favour.

5. Promotion: whether tribunal's decision should be interfered with

Baker v *Cornwall County Council* (1990)
B, who was employed as a technical clerk in the Highways Department, applied in April 1986 for a post as a site surveyor/work checker. She had previously worked as a site technician and had taken a course in construction. Her application was rejected. She applied for two similar posts in November. One post was filled by a man who already carried out the work on a temporary basis. It was considered by C that B was the only

other suitable candidate but that they had advertised in the wrong newspaper. After re-advertising the post three people, including B, were interviewed and a man was appointed to the remaining post. B complained of sex discrimination. Her claim was rejected by the industrial tribunal. She appealed to the EAT; this appeal was dismissed. B appealed on the basis that the tribunal had adopted the wrong approach and had misdirected itself.

The appeal was dismissed. The tribunal's decision could not be interfered with. There was ample evidence to support a finding of sexual discrimination. However, it could not be said that the successful candidate was unqualified for the post and there was evidence to justify the tribunal's findings.

Damages and compensation

1. Damages: discrimination on grounds of sex and race: local authority post at college: industrial tribunal's award of damages: whether appropriate to include exemplary damages

Bradford City Metropolitan Council v *Arora* (1991)
Although such cases are rare, the interviewing of an applicant for a senior post in a local authority college is the exercise of a public function by the authority and is capable of attracting an award of exemplary damages for its abuse.

A, a Sikh, was on the staff of a local authority college. When she applied for the post of head of teaching studies at the college she was not appointed. She complained that she had been unlawfully discriminated against by the council contrary to section 6(1)(a) and (c) and (2)(a) and (b) of the Sex Discrimination Act 1975 and section 4(1)(a) and (c), and (2)(b) and (c) of the Race Relations Act 1976. Her complaints were upheld by the industrial tribunal and she was awarded £500 for hurt feelings. This was increased to £2,000 on review, with £1,000 for exemplary damages. The council appealed against the award of exemplary damages to the EAT. The award was set aside by the EAT on the ground that the selection of individuals for employment by a local authority did not constitute an exercise of public powers in respect of which exemplary damages could be awarded.

A's appeal was allowed and the order of the industrial tribunal restored. The interviewing of an applicant for a senior post in a local authority college was an exercise of a public function by a public authority capable of attracting an award of exemplary damages for its abuse. *Per curiam*, such cases where exemplary damages are justified are probably very rare. The court has to consider the award of compensatory damages including aggravated damages which is not in itself a sufficient punishment. The court or tribunal has to consider whether the conduct which is criticised falls within one of the special categories explained in *Rookes* v *Barnard* and *Cassell & Co* v *Broome* before awarding such damages.

2. Amount of compensation in claim of sex discrimination

Murray v *Powertech (Scotland)* (1992)
When M became pregnant she was dismissed by her employers. Unlawful discrimination was found by the industrial tribunal and compensation awarded to her of £1,313. It was found by the industrial tribunal that there was no evidence to show injury to feelings and they therefore made no order for compensation under this head. M appealed to the EAT.

M's appeal was allowed by the EAT. Injury to feelings was fundamental to a claim of sex discrimination and therefore almost inevitable. The industrial tribunal should have voluntarily considered this aspect and had misdirected itself in failing to make an award for injury to feelings because there had been no evidence shown to prove this.

Key problem areas

- Scope of tribunal's jurisdiction: fresh evidence
- Discovery of documents: circumstances for order
- Time limits: addition of second respondent
- Effect of EC law on time limits rules
- Company take-overs: effect on time limits
- Agreements ousting jurisdiction: effect of EC law
- Public interest immunity
- Bias
- Postponement of hearing: restoration of application
- Powers of EAT to interfere with industrial tribunal finding
- Principles for award of exemplary damages
- Amount of compensation

European Law

Sex discrimination
1. Refusal of employment on grounds of pregnancy
2. Dismissal on grounds of pregnancy-related sickness
3. Dismissal for pregnancy
4. Compensation limits
5. Occupational pension schemes: retirement ages

Equal pay
1. Incremental pay system
2. Incremental pay system: seniority
3. Occupational pension schemes: redundancy
4. Occupational pension schemes: employee's survivor
5. Occupational pension benefits: general principles
6. Occupational pension benefits: common retirement ages
7. Article 119 imposed no obligations in respect of periods of service prior to 17 May 1990
8. Occupational pension schemes: part-time workers
9. Occupational pension benefits: married women
10. Time off for training
11. Job-classification system
12. Part-time worker paid less than full-time
13. Occupational pension scheme: part-time workers
14. State sick pay scheme: part-time workers
15. Collective agreement: part-time workers
16. Unfair dismssal compensation and redundancy pay: part-time workers
17. Part-time workers: discrimination: whether unequal treatment: whether part-time workers treated differently to full-time workers
18. Meaning of "pay": state benefits
19. Age limit for employment
20. Genuine material difference: objective justification

Key problem areas

CHAPTER 7

European Law

European law concerning sex discrimination and equal pay has evolved to a level of extreme complexity. The current law comprises articles of the EC Treaty, directives and a mass of cases heard by the European Court. The impact of much of this European material on the UK system has been direct and dramatic, and has led to changes in UK legislation.

Sex discrimination

The basic provision for sex discrimination is the Equal Treatment Directive 76/207, which governs the implementation of equal treatment for women and men with regard to:

- Access to employment
- Vocational training
- Promotion
- Working conditions

Note that the United Kingdom has an obligation under EC treaties to introduce legislation to fulfil the terms of directives. The significance of EC law for UK sex discrimination is as follows:

1. *Francovich* v *Italian Republic*: individuals affected by a member state's failure to implement directives may claim compensation from the state. The conditions for liability are:

   - The directive contains provisions conferring rights on individuals
   - The content of rights may be ascertained by reference to the provisions of a directive
   - The causal link between damage suffered by individual and breach of obligation by the member state.

2. National tribunals and courts may seek guidance from the European Court.

3. National courts and tribunals have the following powers and duties with respect to EC law:

- Interpretation of domestic legislation in the light of European Court decisions
- An obligation to interpret domestic legislation with reference to EC directives
- The power to consider the implication of EC directives where the claimant has not raised the point of EC law.

4. Individual employees may seek direct enforcement of EU Directives only where employers provide public service under state control. This has been widely defined and includes, for example, the British Gas Corporation before privatisation, health authorities and universities.

The following are examples of case law.

1. Refusal of employment on grounds of pregnancy

Dekker v *Stichting Vormingscentrum voor Jonge Volwassenen Plus* (1991)
D, who was pregnant, applied for a job. She was refused employment despite the fact that she was the most suitable candidate. The employer refused to engage her because she would be entitled to maternity benefits which the employer would have to pay. D claimed that this amounted to a breach of the Dutch law which implemented the EC Equal Treatment Directive. The matter was referred to the European Court, which decided:

1. There had been a direct contravention of articles 2(1) and 3(1) of the Directive.
2. The motive for refusal to employ had been the fact that D was pregnant. This could only apply to women and was directly discriminatory.
3. Financial grounds did not justify the discrimination.

2. Dismissal on grounds of pregnancy-related sickness

Handels-og Kontorfunktionaererenes Forbund i Danmark v *Dansk Arbeijdsgiverforening (acting for AldiMarked K/S)* (1991)
H took 100 days' sick leave during her pregnancy and confinement. She was dismissed. She claimed sex discrimination in the Danish courts. The

question was referred to the European Court. H argued that there had been sex discrimination because male employees could not have been treated in the way in which she had been treated. The European Court made the following rulings:

1. Dismissal for pregnancy was direct discrimination.
2. Dismissal of a female for sickness reasons not related to pregnancy was not discriminatory provided that a male would be treated in the same way.
3. The Directive did not preclude dismissals for pregnancy-related absence where such absence occurred after maternity leave. There was no direct discrimination where a man would have been dismissed under similar conditions.

Dismissal for pregnancy

Webb v EMO Air Cargo (UK) (1992)
To dismiss a woman who is unable to carry out her duties due to pregnancy is not contrary to the Sex Discrimination Act 1975 in circumstances where a man would also be dismissed if he was absent for a similar amount of time due to a different medical reason.

After being engaged to cover a period of employment when the permanent post-holder would be absent on maternity leave, W became pregnant. She was dismissed and brought an action against her employer claiming sex discrimination.

As she was unavailable to work through the period for which she had been engaged, the pregnancy was not the prime cause of her dismissal. However, the matter was referred to the European Court to determine whether it is discriminatory to dismiss a woman who is unable to carry out a job for the period for which she has been engaged due to pregnancy. The European Court ruled:

1. Dismissal of a pregnant woman on the basis that she would not be able to perform her duties on a temporary basis could not be justified.
2. There could be no comparison of a woman incapable through pregnancy with a man incapable for medical or other reasons.
3. There was a clear distinction between pregnancy and illness.
4. Protection given to pregnant women by EC law was not affected by the fact that a woman's presence was essential for the business to operate properly.

5. The fact that the claimant was a maternity leave replacement did not affect the ruling.

4. Compensation limits

Marshall v *Southampton and South West Hampshire Area Health Authority (No 2)* (1993)

M's sex discrimination claim was upheld and the matter remitted to an industrial tribunal for compensation to be assessed. Total compensation was assessed at approximately £19,000. The statutory limit for compensation at the time was £6,250.

The tribunal refused to apply this limit on the basis that it would render compensation inadequate and was thus in breach of article 6 of the Equal Treatment Directive. Article 6 provides, in paraphrase, that member states are obliged to introduce measures necessary to enable persons who consider themselves wronged by failure to apply the principle of equal treatment, to pursue their claims by judicial process.

The employers appealed against this ruling. The matter was referred to the European Court by the House of Lords. The decision was as follows:

1. Where the objective of a directive was to be secured by compensation, this must make good the loss actually sustained.
2. Where appropriate, this should include an award of interest.
3. The statutory limit for compensation under UK law could not amount to proper implementation of the directive.
4. Individuals can rely directly upon article 6 to set aside statutory limits on compensation.

5. Occupational pension schemes: retirement ages

Roberts v *Tate & Lyle Industries* (1986)

The complainant belonged to an occupational pension scheme which provided for compulsory retirement for men at age 65 and women at age 60. Both received pensions. The company provided, under its compulsory redundancy terms, that both men and wonen could receive an immediate early pension at age 55.

Ms R was made redundant at the age of 53 and therefore did not receive a pension. She claimed that the scheme was in breach of the equal treatment principle because men could be paid a pension ten years before their normal retirement age whereas women could only receive one five years before. In the European Court's view, it was not contrary to the Equal

Treatment Directive for employers to arrange for both men and women who were made redundant to receive a pension at 55 years of age. This did not amount to sex discrimination even though the result might be that men would receive pensions at a time earlier in relation to their normal pensionable age than that applicable to women.

Equal pay

Article 119 of the EC Treaty establishes the principle of equal pay for equal work. This rule can be directly enforced in UK tribunals and courts. Article 119 provides, in paraphrase:

1. Member states shall ensure and maintain the application of the principle that men and women should receive equal pay for equal work.
2. "Pay" means the ordinary basic or minimum wage or salary and any other consideration, whether in cash or kind, which the worker receives, directly or indirectly, in respect of his employment.
3. Equal pay without discrimination based on sex means:

   - Pay for the same work at piece rates must be calculated on the basis of the same unit of measurement.
   - Pay for work at time rates shall be the same for the same job.

A major problem with the application of this rule is the situation where the work performed by men and women is different, but is alleged to be of the same value. The problem was addressed by EEC Directive 75/117 whch imposed a positive obligation on member states to ensure that the equal pay principle was observed.

Examples of European case law in this area are as follows.

1. Incremental pay system

Handels-og Konterfunktionaerernes Forbund i Danmark v Dansk Arbejdsgiverforening (acting for Danfoss) (1989)
The Danish Union of Commercial and Clerical Employees made a claim against Danfoss, the employer, before the Industrial Arbitration Board. Danfoss paid the same basic wages to all employees in the same wage group. It also awarded pay supplements which were based on mobility, seniority, and training.

The Union brought the case on behalf of two female employees. Each worked within a different wage group. Within the two groups it was shown that a man's average wage was higher than a woman's.

The European Court made the following rulings:

1. The system of pay supplements was such that women could not discover the reasons for differences between their pay and that of men in the same wage group.
2. It was for an employer to prove that its practice in the matter of wages was not discriminatory where a female worker established, in relation to a relatively large number of employees, that the average pay for women was less than for men.
3. In order to show that its practice in the matter of wages did not work to the disadvantage of female employees, the employer must show how it has applied criteria concerning pay supplements and will thus be forced to make the pay system transparent.

Incremental pay system: seniority

Nimz v *Freie und Hansestadt Hamburg* (1991)
N was employed for 20 hours a week. Her terms of employment provided that she could move up the salary scale after six years' service if she worked at least 75% of normal working hours. Employees working less than 75% had to work for 12 years to receive the increase. Women comprised more than 90% of employees working under 75% of normal hours. N claimed that these terms were in breach of article 119.

The European Court decision was as follows: .

1. The terms of employment were in breach of article 119 unless the employer could show objective justification by factors unrelated to sex discrimination.
2. The argument that full-time workers acquired skills more quickly and were more experienced was not, in the present case, objective and unrelated to sex discrimination.
3. It was for the national court to decide whether provisions in a collective agreement, such as in the present case, were justified by objective and non-discriminatory factors.

3. Occupational pension schemes: redundancy

Barber v *Guardian Royal Exchange Assurance Group* (1990)
B, an employee of G, was made redundant at the age of 52. B belonged to

G's occupational pension scheme which was regarded as a "contracted-out" scheme for the purposes of UK social security legislation. This meant that members of the scheme would contractually waive the earnings-related part of the state pension scheme.

B argued that the terms of his redundancy which related to entitlement to an early retirement pension were in breach of article 119. The redundancy terms provided that women would be entitled to an immediate pension on reaching the age of 50 whereas the relevant age for a man was 55.

The question for the European Court was whether redundancy-related benefits fell within the scope of article 119 or EEC Directive 75/117. Its ruling was as follows:

1. Contracted-out private occupational pension schemes which are wholly financed by employers and/or workers without contributions from public authorities count as "pay" because they are part of the consideration offered to workers by employers.
2. Pensions paid under contracted-out schemes fall within the concept of "pay".
3. It was contrary to article 119 to impose an age condition which differed according to sex in respect of pensions paid under a contracted-out scheme.
4. The equal pay principle applied to each element of remuneration granted to women or to men.
5. Article 119 could be relied on in proceedings before national courts.
6. This ruling did not apply to claims prior to 17 May 1990 unless legal proceedings had already been initiated.

4. Occupational pension schemes: employee's survivor

Ten Oever v Stichting Bedrijfpensioenfonds voor het Glazenwassers en Schoonmaakbedrijf (1993)

1. Equality in respect of occupational pensions can only be claimed in respect of benefits payable for periods of employment after 17 May, 1990.
2. This is subject to the exception in favour of workers or persons claiming under them who have inititiated proceedings or made claims under relevant national law.
3. Article 119 covers pension benefits payable to an employee's

survivor, because the crucial factor is that the pension is paid by reason of the employment relationship.

5. Occupational pension benefits: general principles

Coloroll Pension Trustees v *Russell and Others* (C-200/91), (1994)
The Coloroll Group of companies collapsed in 1990. Trustees of the group's pension funds sought guidance on the application of article 119 to the rules set out in the various pension schemes. The European Court gave the following guidance:

1. Article 119 could be relied upon by both employees and their dependants against pension trustees as well as against employers.
2. Trustees have a duty to use all means available to eliminate discrimination in pay.
3. Implementation of article 119 involves the levelling up of rights of disadvantaged groups to those of advantaged groups.
4. This relates to periods of service between the finding of discrimination and the introduction of measures to eliminate discrimination.
5. As regards service subsequent to this, article 119 does not preclude measures to achieve equality which include reduction of the advantaged group's rights.
6. The rule in *Barber* concerning time limits also applies in respect of survivors' benefits. But it is only applicable to benefits not linked to length of service (for example death in service benefits) where the operative event occurred before 17 May 1990.
7. In relation to occupational pension benefits, article 119 does not apply where:

   ● additional voluntary contributions (AVCs) are paid by employees;
   ● these AVCs are credited to a separate fund;
   ● the occupational pension scheme does no more than provide an administrative framework.

8. Where an inequality of employers' contributions to benefit schemes arises from the use of actuarial factors, this does not come within article 119.
9. In cases where pension rights are transferred from one employer to another, the transferee must increase benefits in order to eliminate

discriminatory treatment so far as such benefits are payable for periods of service after 17 May 1990.

6. Occupational pension benefits: common retirement ages

Smith and others v *Avdel Systems Ltd* (1994)
S and others were members of an occupational pension scheme which set retirement ages of 60 for women and 65 for men. On 1 July 1991, a common retirement age of 65 was introduced. One consequence of this was that women retiring between the ages of 60 and 65 had their pensions reduced by 4% for each year preceding their 65th birthday.

S and others made an equal pay claim. The industrial tribunal referred the matter to the European Court for a ruling on whether it was consistent with article 119 to adopt a common retirement age of 65 for women and men, despite the fact that this led to adverse consequences for women. The European Court made the following points:

1. Article 119 operated to preclude employers from raising retirement ages for women to that of men for periods of service between 17 May 1990 and the date upon which retirement ages were equalised.
2. In relation to periods of service completed after the date on which retirement ages were equalised, article 119 did not preclude measures which aimed to achieve equal treatment by reducing the rights of the advantaged group.
3. Article 119 imposed no obligations in respect of periods of service prior to 17 May 1990.

7. Occupational pension benefits: transitional arrangements

Van den Akker and others v *Stichting Shell Pensioenfonds* (C-28/93) (1994)
An employer equalised retirement ages for men and women at the age of 60. Transitional arrangements were introduced to allow female employees to retire at 55.

After the ruling in *Barber*, the rules of the pension scheme were amended to repeal the transitional arrangements from 1 June 1991. The question of this repeal was referred to the European Court, which ruled as follows:

1. Article 119 does not allow the retention of special rules in relation to one gender after the date on which a common retirement age has been introduced.

2. For periods of service completed between 17 May 1990 and the date on which uniform retirement ages are implemented, article 119 does not permit the achievement of equality other than by applying the same arrangements to men and to women.

8. Occupational pension schemes: part-time workers

Vroege v *NCIV Instituut voor Volkshuisvesting BV and Stichting Pensioenfonds NCIV* (C-57/93) (1994)
V, a part-time worker, was excluded by the rules of the employer's pension scheme. On 1 January 1991 new rules came into force which permitted part-timers to join the scheme from that date. V claimed a retroactive right to join the scheme from 1976. The question was referred to the European Court, with the following results:

1. Article 119 applied to the right to join an occupational pension scheme.
2. In relation to the exclusion of part-time workers, article 119 was contravened where such exclusion affected more women than men, unless the employer could show objective justification.
3. The temporal effect of the decision in *Barber* did not apply to the right to join a pension scheme.
4. The direct effect of article 119 could be relied upon from 1976.

9. Occupational pension benefits: married women

Fisscher v *Voorhuis Henelo BV and Stichting Bedrijfspensioenfonds voor de Detailhandel* (1994)
An employer's pension scheme excluded married women. These rules were changed in 1991. F, a married woman, was admitted to membership. She claimed the right to have retroactive membership from 1978 when her employment had begun. On a reference to the European Court, the court held:

1. The exclusion of married women from a pension scheme amounted to direct sex discrimination.
2. The ruling in *Barber* had limited the right to equal treatment in pension rights to periods of service subsequent to 17 May 1990. But this did not apply to the right to membership. Article 119 could be relied on with effect from 1976.

3. The fact that employees could make retroactive claims to join occupational pension schemes did not allow employees to avoid paying contributions covering the period of membership claimed.
4. National rules covering time limits for bringing proceedings could be relied upon with reference to employees asserting their rights to membership of pension schemes, provided that they did not render the exercise of rights practically impossible.

10. Time off for training courses

Arbeiterwohlfahrt der Stadt Berlin EV v Botel (1992)
Ms B was a part-time nurse. She was a member of the Staff Committee at her workplace. German law provided that members of such Committees had to be given paid time off work to attend training courses. Ms B attended six of them. These exceeded her normal working hours. She was paid for her normal working hours but not for her own time spent on the courses.

Full-time workers who attended such courses were paid their normal salary. Ms B claimed for compensation of paid leave or paid overtime. The question was referred to the European Court. The decision was as follows:

1. Paid leave or overtime paid for the purpose of attending training courses was "pay" for the purposes of article 119.
2. It was contrary to article 119 where national law deprived part-time employees of paid leave or paid overtime up to the limit of hours of work in force for full-time employees.
3. This principle applied where there were more women than men in part-time work unless the member state in question could show that the national legislation was justified by objective factors unrelated to sex discrimination.

11. Job-classification system

Commission v United Kingdom (1982)
The Commission complained of the United Kingdom's failure to implement Directive 75/117. In particular, it was alleged that the UK had not introduced a job-classification system which would help to determine whether work was "of equal value" with other work. The Equal Pay Act 1970 provided that such a system could only be introduced with the employer's consent. Further, the 1970 Act made no other provision for ways of determining equal value.

The European Court ruled as follows:

1. It is primarily the responsibility of member states to ensure the application of the principle of equal pay for work of equal value.
2. Where there is disagreement as to the application of the concept, employees must have a right to claim before an appropriate authority and to have their rights acknowledged by a binding decision.
3. It is not sufficient for a member state to leave it to employers to determine what amounts to equal work of equal value.

12. Part-time worker paid less than full-time

Jenkins v *Kingsgate (Clothing Productions) Ltd* (1980)
Ms J, a part-time worker, claimed that the fact that she was paid a lower hourly rate than her full-time male colleagues who did exactly the same work was a breach of the equal pay principle. She brought proceedings in an industrial tribunal under the Equal Pay Act 1970, arguing in particular that she was employed on "like work" with men in the same employment.

The employer argued that the different rates of pay were due to a material difference other than the difference of sex. The European Court made the following points:

1. Differences in pay prohibited by article 119 are exclusively those based on the difference of sex.
2. The fact that part-time work is paid less than full-time is not in itself discriminatory.
3. If it is established that a considerably smaller percentage of women than men perform the minimum number of weekly hours in order to claim the full rate of pay, this is contrary to article 119.
4. It is for the national courts to decide whether or not a pay policy such as that in the present case is discriminatory. Regard must be had to:

   ● The facts of the case
   ● The history of the case
   ● The employer's intention. This may be, for example, an endeavour on justifiable economic grounds to encourage full-time working regardless of discrimination based on sex.

13. Occupational pension scheme: part-time workers

Bilka-Kaufhaus GmbH v *Karin Weber von Harz* (1986)

B, a department store, had established an occupational pension scheme for its workers. The scheme applied to part-time workers only if they had worked full-time for at least 15 out of a total of 20 years.

Ms Weber was not eligible for a pension. She claimed that the rules discriminated against her on the grounds of her sex, because female workers were more likely than their male colleagues to take part-time work so that they could look after their children. The German court referred the matter to the European Court, which ruled as follows:

1. If it should be found that a much lower proportion of women than men worked full time, then the exclusion of part-timers from the scheme would be a breach of article 119.
2. Where an undertaking was able to show that its pay practice could be explained by objectively justified factors unrelated to sex discrimination, then there would be no breach of article 119.

B had argued that its exclusion of part-time workers from the pension scheme was aimed to discourage part-time work. The reason for this was that part-time workers generally refused to work late in the afternoon and on Saturdays. It was therefore necessary to make full-time work more attractive than part-time.

It was for the national court to decide whether the reasons put forward by employers for pay practices could be justified on economic grounds. If a national court finds that the measures chosen by an employer:

- corresponded to a real need on the part of an undertaking,
- were appropriate with a view to achieving the objectives pursued, and
- were necessary to that end,

then the fact that the measures affected a far greater number of women than men is not sufficient to show that they constitute an infringement of article 119.

14. State sick pay scheme: part-time workers

Rinner-Kühn v *FWW Spezial-Gebäudereinigung GmbH* (1989)

R was employed as an office cleaner for ten hours a week. She made a complaint against her employer on the basis that she had been refused wages during absence from work because of sickness.

The relevant German legislation provided that employers must provide sick pay for up to six weeks: employees who worked no more than ten hours a week were excluded. The national court asked the European Court for a ruling on whether such legislation was compatible with article 119 and Directive 75/117. The court ruled as follows:

1. The proportion of women adversely affected by the exclusion was considerably greater than that of men.
2. This resulted in discrimination against female workers.
3. The position would be different only if the distinction between the two categories of employee was justified by objective factors unrelated to sex discrimination.
4. If the member state could show that the means chosen met a necessary aim of social policy and that they were suitable and requisite for attaining that aim, then the mere fact that the provision affected a much greater number of females than males could not be regarded as infringing article 119.

15. Collective agreement: part-time workers

Kowalska v *Freie und Hansestadt Hamburg* (1990)
K, an employee of Hamburg City, challenged her employer's refusal to award her a severance grant on her retirement. Only full-time employees were entitled to such grants. It was accepted that there were many more part-time females than males. The European Court's view was that there had been a prima facie infringement of article 119 but it was up to the national court to decide whether this could be objectively justified.

16. Unfair dismissal compensation and redundancy pay: part-time workers

R v *Secretary of State for Employment, ex p Equal Opportunities Commission* (1994)
Statutory qualifying thresholds which exclude part time employees from compensation for unfair dismissal and redundancy payments are incompatible with EC law. Because considerably more women than men work part time, the Secretary of State was requested by the Equal Opportunities Commission to reconsider statutory provisions which excluded part-time employees from compensation for unfair dismissal and

redundancy payments as these discriminated against women and therefore conflicted with EC law.

A letter was received from the Secretary of State replying that the statutory thresholds were justified. The Commission applied for judicial review. D had been employed part-time by a health authority and had been unable to claim compensation after being made redundant due to the statutory thresholds. D was joined as a party.

The application was dismissed by the Divisional Court and an appeal to the Court of Appeal was dismissed. On further appeal to the House of Lords, it was held:

1. Assuming the statutory thresholds were in conflict with EC law, D's claim to redundancy pay should properly be brought against her employer in the industrial tribunal.
2. The Commission had a sufficient interest in the proceedings to give it the necessary locus standi by virtue of section 53(1) of the Sex Discrimination Act 1975.
3. The Divisional Court had jurisdiction to declare that primary legislation was incompatible with EC law under RSC, Order 52, rule 1(2). The Commission's appeal was allowed.
4. The onus was on the Secretary of State to show that the threshold provisions were objectively justified and thus did not infringe article 119 of the Treaty. As this had not been shown on the evidence before the Divisional Court, declarations should be made that the provisions were incompatible with article 119 and the relevant EC directives.

As a result of this decision, the Employment Protection (Part-time Employees) Regulations 1995 were introduced. These Regulations remove the provisions of the Employment Protection (Consolidation) Act 1978 and the Trade Union and Labour Relations (Consolidation) Act 1992 which excluded part-time workers from entitlement to rights under those statutes.

17. Part-time workers: discrimination: whether unequal treatment: whether part-time workers treated differently to full-time workers

Helmig v *Stadt Lengerich* (1995)
Female part-time workers in Germany were the plaintiffs and the German courts asked the European Court of Justice for a preliminary ruling under article 177 of the EEC Treaty. The plaintiffs claimed that the restriction in

collective agreements which provided that payments would only be granted for overtime which was worked in excess of normal full-time working hours was discriminatory and thus in breach of the Treaty. The European Court ruled as follows:

1. There had been no unequal treatment or discrimination in this case.
2. The part-time workers received the same overall pay as full-time workers for the same number of hours worked.
3. Part-time workers were entitled to the same overtime pay as full-time workers if they worked more than the normal working hours of full-time workers.
4. In order for there to be unequal treatment the overall pay of full-time workers had to be higher than that of part-time workers for the same number of hours worked.

18. Meaning of "pay": state benefits

Defrenne v *Belgium* (1971)
A Belgian law dealing with retirement pensions exluded air hostesses from its scope. The pensions were financed by contributions from workers and employers, and by state subsidy. D argued that there was a necessary and direct link between salaries and retirement pensions, because some conditions of employment directly influenced the amount of the pension.

It was argued on behalf of the Commission that social security benefits in general, and pensions in particular, must be excluded from the scope of article 119. The European Court ruled:

1. Article 119 provides that member states are required to ensure the application of the principle of equal pay for equal work.
2. "Pay" means any consideration, whether in cash or kind, immediate or future, provided that the employee receives it in respect of his employment.
3. Social security schemes cannot be brought into this concept.
4. The part due from employers to finance social security schemes does not amount to a direct or indirect payment to an employee.

19. Age limit for employment

Defrenne v *Sabena (No 3)* (1978)
D, a female air stewardess, argued that her employers had been in breach of

article 119 in compulsorily terminating her employment at age 40 when no such condition applied to male stewards. The European Court ruled that:

1. Article 119 was limited to the question of pay discrimination between men and women workers.
2. This constituted a special rule, the application of which was linked to precise factors.
3. The fact that the fixing of certain conditions of employment, for example a special age limit, might have pecuniary consequences, did not bring such conditions within the scope of article 119.

20. Genuine material difference: objective justification

Enderby v *Frenchay Health Authority and Secretary of State for Health* (1993)
An equal value claim was made by E, a senior speech therapist. She appealed against the tribunal's decision that her employer had established a material factor defence under section 1(3) of the Equal Pay Act 1970 by showing that the difference in pay between her and her male comparators resulted from the bargaining structure of the NHS Council which established scales of pay, and the structures within the separate professions of E and her male comparators. The decision was upheld by the EAT.

The Court of Appeal held that the case would be referred to the European Court of Justice. The tribunal had not addressed the issue of whether the variation was appropriate and necessary when it had considered whether it was objectively justified. This question of whether it was necessary to justify the whole or only part of a variation was a question of general importance which should be determined by the European Court.

It was also necessary for the European Court to decide on the issue of whether an employer could defend a claim of unintentional indirect discrimination by proving the absence of any condition which prevented a woman from becoming a member of a privileged group, without having to prove an objective justification for a difference in terms. The European Court ruled:

1. A prima facie case of discrimination is raised where valid statistics disclose differences in pay between two jobs, one of which is carried out exclusively by men and the other by women. The burden is then upon the employer to show that there are objective reasons for the differences.

2. Objective justification is not established by the fact that differing pay rates were the result of non-discriminatory collective bargaining processes.
3. The role of the national court is to determine to what extent a shortage of candidates for a job amounts to objective justification.
4. Where a national court is able to ascertain the precise proportion of the difference in pay which is attributable to market forces, then this will justify the difference in pay to the extent of that proportion.

Key problem areas

- Significance of EC law: whether directly applicable
- Refusal of employment on grounds of pregnancy
- Pregnancy-related sickness and dismissal
- Statutory compensation limits
- Retirement ages: pension schemes
- Meaning of "pay" for purposes of article 119
- Incremental pay system: whether discriminatory
- Redundancy: occupational pension schemes
- Occupational pension schemes: survivor of employee; general principles; part-time workers
- Common retirement ages: effect of article 119
- Occupational pension benefits: married women: retroactive claims
- Equal pay: time off for training courses; job classification system; meaning of "pay": state benefits
- Position of part-time workers paid less than full-time
- State sick-pay scheme: position of part-time workers
- Part-time workers: collective agreements; unfair dismissal compensation and redundancy pay
- Age limit for employment
- Genuine material difference: justification

Index

objective justification, 78-79
incremental pay system, 66-67
job classification system, 72-73
occupational pension schemes,
    65-66, 67-72
    common retirement ages, 70
    employer's survivor, 68-69
    general principles, 69-70
    married women, 71
    part-time workers, 71, 74
    transitional arrangements, 70-
        71
part-time worker paid less than
    full-time, 73
part-time workers, 75-77
pay, meaning, 77
redundancy pay,
    part-time workers, 75-76
refusal of employment on
    grounds of pregnancy, 63
sex discrimination, 62-66
significance, 62-63
state sick pay scheme, 74-75
time off for training courses, 72
unfair dismissal compensation,
    part-time workers, 75-76
Exceptions, 24-25
Exclusions, 24-25

Genuine occupational qualification,
    preservation of decency, 24

Industrial tribunal practice and
    procedure, 51-59
    compensation, 58-59
    complaints, 52
    damages, 58-59
    discovery of documents, 55
    EAT jurisdiction, 52-53
    interference with decision of
        tribunal, 57-58

jurisdiction, 55-56
public interest immunity, 56
restoration of application, 57
time limits, 53-55
    addition of second respondent,
        53
    company take-over, 54-55
    redundancy payments, 54

Legislation,
    background to, 2
Less favourable treatment,
    female nurse refusing to wear
        cap, 24

Mobility clause,
    justification, 7

Pregnancy, 27-33
    assessment of compensation,
        30-32
    comparison with male employee,
        28, 29, 30
    evidence of treatment of male
        employee, 29
    misconduct, and, 28-29
    unmarried school matron
        dismissed, 32

Redundancy selection
    part-time employees first, 20-21
Requirement or condition of
    employment, 15-20
    advert for graduate aged 27-35,
        18-19
    age requirement, 16-17
    fewer women than men able to
        comply, 19, 22
    only part-time employees made
        redundant, 17-18

SEX
DISCRIMINATION
AT WORK